T0354637

Praise for *The Five-Day Leader*
by Lyle Wells

Lyle Wells is a "leader's leader" and one of my heroes. *The Five-Day Leader* is filled with practical wisdom for vocational and lay Christian leaders who want to make a greater kingdom impact. I found myself saying "that's so true" after every chapter. This book will help you grow and build great teams … guaranteed!

—*Lt. Gen. Van Antwerp, U.S. Army (Ret.), former Chief of the U.S. Army Corps of Engineers*

At his heart, Lyle is an encourager. You feel like he is walking beside you in his writing. He never talks down to you. Nothing is glib. He's a very careful and prayerful thinker. It's always worth your time to consider his ideas. He knows this road very well. I invite you to let him walk with you through *The Five-Day Leader*.

—*Bishop Gregory O. Brewer, Episcopal Bishop of Central Florida*

No matter your vocational field or educational level, influence and impact don't come without challenges and, thankfully, joys. Leadership ain't easy, but it is worth it. Lyle Wells is an outstanding leader and has written a superb resource for us to learn from. With engaging stories and real-time application, you will be encouraged and challenged by *The Five-Day Leader*.

—*Gregg Matte, Pastor, Houston's First Baptist Church*

The Five-Day Leader is the real deal for growing your managers. We have used this curriculum and have seen powerful, significant growth in our team. Use it and your people and your organization will grow too!

—*Mike Rovner, Entrepreneur, Founder of Thrive Teaching, Author of* Supernatural Business

I've been watching Lyle coach and lead for over twenty-five years. *The Five-Day Leader* is a powerful yet easy-to-read culmination of Lyle's wisest advice and best how-tos. If you are looking to grow yourself or your team, this is a must-read!

—*Kadi Cole, Best-Selling Author, Leadership Coach, Business Consultant*

As a coach, I understand the importance of "process" in developing a championship program. I am pleased and proud to see that my friend Lyle Wells has embraced the celebration of process in *The Five-Day Leader*. Lyle has been a voice of wisdom to my teams and a constant source of influence in my own life. This book will be like a great workout—full of challenges, opportunities to develop new habits, and benefits that will last a lifetime.

—*Billy Kennedy, SEC 2016 Men's Basketball Coach of the Year*

Coach Wells directly changed my life on and off the basketball court, instilling some of the principles and values I currently have and teach to my children. Coach gave *accountability* meaning. It meant being accountable for your actions on and off the court. Coach helped guide and shape me and other players he coached into the guys we are today.

—*Eddie Willingham, Sr. Manager, Inventory Planning*
& E-Commerce, Las Vegas Raiders

Lyle Wells is simply amazing! He has the uncanny ability to take a subject and present it in a way that is understandable, applicable, and heartfelt. There is no doubt that this process will help leaders become more intentional in making an impact on the people they serve. As a husband, father, and coach, I know these habits will undoubtedly have a positive effect on my family and team.

—*Eric McDade, Head Basketball Coach,*
Midway High School, Waco, Texas

The Five-Day Leader is packed with leadership wisdom and strategic insights not designed in the ivory tower but on the turf and in the trenches of lessons learned the hard way. Bottom line, when Lyle speaks, I always take notes. Always practical, he has a gift for not just giving accurate answers but asking the right questions. I am a more inspired and effective leader because of him.

—*Bernie Cueto, PhD, Vice President for Spiritual*
Development, Campus Pastor, Associate Professor Biblical and
Theological Studies, Palm Beach Atlantic University

In his candid, profound, and accessible style, Lyle Wells has written a must-read book for leaders passionate about growth and relentless about reaching their full potential. *The Five-Day Leader* will encourage, challenge, and equip you with the tools you need to make maximum impact in leadership and ministry. This book is not about a short-term approach but about shaping lifelong habits that will impact the church and world for generations to come.

—*Banning Liebscher, Jesus Culture, Founder and Pastor*

Lyle Wells is a master coach *par excellence* who speaks from years of experience and decades of leadership engagement. Lyle's straightforward words will challenge you to raise the bar and expand your leadership parameters. *The Five-Day Leader* will give you both fundamental skills and a game-day strategy for your sphere of influence. Buy this book! Read each chapter; take notes. Put what you learn into practice. You will not regret it. How do I know this? Because Lyle Wells *is* my executive coach.

—*Dr. Mark Yarbrough, President, Dallas Theological Seminary*

When Lyle Wells talks, I listen. He has a unique ability to deliver trajectory-shaping truth in a way that is enjoyable, encouraging, and empowering. I trust many will find this resource to be a timely bump out of a discouraging leadership rut. I am a better leader because of Lyle Wells and trust you will soon be feeling the same way.

—*Timothy Ateek, Teaching Pastor, Watermark Community Church*

As a coach, I love a *great* game plan. Thank you, Lyle, for providing detailed insights and a practical plan to grow my influence through Relentless Growth, Ridiculous Routines, and Resilient Relationships. I can't wait to use *The Five-Day Leader* guide and watch my "next year me" be a better coach, leader, friend, and Christ-follower than my "this year me."

—*Kamie Ethridge, Head Women's Basketball Coach,*
Washington State University, 1988 Olympic Gold Medalist,
1986 NCAA Champion, and Wade Trophy Winner

THE
FIVE-DAY
LEADER

AN INSANELY PRACTICAL GUIDE FOR
RELENTLESS GROWTH, RIDICULOUS ROUTINES,
AND RESILIENT RELATIONSHIPS.

LYLE WELLS

WESTBOW
PRESS®
A DIVISION OF THOMAS NELSON
& ZONDERVAN

WestBow Press books may be ordered through booksellers or by contacting:

WestBow Press
A Division of Thomas Nelson & Zondervan
1663 Liberty Drive
Bloomington, IN 47403
www.westbowpress.com
844-714-3454

Because of the dynamic nature of the internet, any web addresses or links contained in this book may have changed since publication and may no longer be valid. The views expressed in this work are solely those of the author and do not necessarily reflect the views of the publisher, and the publisher hereby disclaims any responsibility for them.

Any people depicted in stock imagery provided by Getty Images are models, and such images are being used for illustrative purposes only. Certain stock imagery © Getty Images.

All Scripture quotations unless otherwise noted are taken from The Holy Bible, New International Version® NIV® Copyright © 1973 1978 1984 2011 by Biblica, Inc. TM. Used by permission. All rights reserved worldwide.

Scripture quotations marked NKJV are taken from the New King James Version® Copyright © 1982 by Thomas Nelson. Used by permission. All rights reserved.

Scripture quotations marked (NLT) are taken from the Holy Bible, New Living Translation, copyright ©1996, 2004, 2015 by Tyndale House Foundation. Used by permission of Tyndale House Publishers, a Division of Tyndale House Ministries, Carol Stream, Illinois 60188. All rights reserved.

ISBN: 978-1-6642-6988-0 (sc)
ISBN: 978-1-6642-6989-7 (hc)
ISBN: 978-1-6642-6987-3 (e)

Library of Congress Control Number: 2022911509

Print information available on the last page.

WestBow Press rev. date: 7/14/2022

To Ronda, Michael, and Jordie,
your amazing love and support have
helped me to dream big dreams,
pursue every one of them,
and live a life full of adventure, challenge, and growth.

CONTENTS

FOREWORD

When Lyle asked me to write the foreword for this book, there was no way I was going to decline! Lyle has not only been a dear friend to our family but also to our Messenger International team. He has coached us both individually and corporately, speaking to our teams at fundraising events and in online courses. He has also helped us navigate major transitions and shifts in our organization—empowering us to grow and expand our influence and impact.

Having been personally impacted by Lyle's leadership coaching, I'm thrilled that he has written this book. In *The Five-Day Leader*, Lyle shares his proven leadership lessons that have not only revolutionized my life, but also lives of leaders in ministry, education, corporations, athletic teams, and nonprofit organizations. Lyle consistently reminds us that "intentionality brings increase." So, to increase your influence and credibility as a leader, you must become intentional about growing as one.

In the pages that follow, Lyle will guide you through a simple process that will equip you to maximize your platforms—whether that's at the kitchen table surrounded by your family, in the classroom before your students, in the boardroom gathered with your executives, or even on a stage before thousands. Growth energizes and prepares us for new challenges while inspiring those we lead to grow as well.

The most influential leaders are committed to personal growth, and they are consistently learning, applying, and acquiring new tools and ways of influencing those they lead and care deeply about. Before you turn the page, however, I must warn you: You will be challenged. You will be stretched. You will be provoked. But the rewards and benefits of the process will far outweigh the pain of it. Embrace the process!

—John Bevere
Minister, Best-Selling Author,
Cofounder of Messenger International and MessengerX

FIRST HALF

THE FUNDAMENTALS

CHAPTER 1

OVERWHELMED AND
UNDERRESOURCED

In the airplane seats beside and behind me were the ten players of Palm Beach Atlantic University's (PBAU) basketball team. These young men ranged in age from eighteen to twenty-one, not that much older than my own children, and I felt immense responsibility for each one of them.

As the flight attendant began the preflight safety briefing in Spanish, I did one last count to make sure everyone had made it onto the plane. Most of them were already asleep, and I planned on joining them shortly.

Every other year, we took our college team on an international trip. This particular year, we'd gone to Bolivia, a landlocked country between Brazil and Chile. We'd been in the capital city of La Paz for a week, practicing and playing against Bolivian university teams. The trip was also a service opportunity, so we'd worked with Centro de Vida, a boy's orphanage. We ate there, slept there, and whenever we weren't playing basketball, served the boys of the orphanage by playing games, completing repairs at the facility, and going into the city at night to bring food, blankets, and socks to children living on the streets. In fact, we'd ministered in the city straight through our final night, ensuring we'd sleep through the nonstop, ten-hour flight back to Miami.

Satisfied that everyone was accounted for, I settled into my seat with that "good tired" feeling. All of us were fast asleep before the plane even left the ground.

Suddenly, I was woken by a rough landing. I was confused, certain the flight had passed too quickly. Checking my watch, I saw that we'd only left La Paz a few hours before. Something was not right. When I opened the window shade and saw we were approaching an unfamiliar terminal, my heart started to race, and I wondered if we'd gotten on the wrong plane. As we pulled into a gate, I received some startling news—we were in Brazil, not Miami!

I was nearly in panic mode as we exited the plane into a country that I knew very little about. I was a basketball coach, not a seasoned traveler. I knew how to create game plans and motivate twenty-year-olds, not how to navigate customs and international travel.

I needed information. Hoping my four years of high school Spanish would be enough, I approached the gate agent. First, I tried English. No response. I tried Spanish next. No response. Then I remembered Brazil is a Portuguese-speaking nation, and I didn't know a word of Portuguese.

Stuck in a foreign country, unable to communicate, without proper visas for Brazil—and I was supposed to be in charge. I was as frightened as I'd ever been. My players were looking to me for answers, and I had none to give them. Looking back, I've come to realize I was *over*whelmed and *under*resourced!

I didn't lack motivation—my entire heart was to protect my team and to provide for their needs, immediate and long term—but I lacked the skills, tools, information, and resources I needed. I didn't speak Portuguese. I was in a chaotic airport with no sense of direction, and I had no idea where to go for information (this was long before iPhones and Google). I lacked any understanding of why we had landed there, let alone of international travel laws and customs. I didn't have any Brazilian money, only US dollars and a few bolivianos we'd kept as souvenirs. It was a horrible feeling, bearing that much responsibility to my boys and their parents but feeling completely overwhelmed and underresourced. All I could do was pray in the middle of that crowded terminal.

I eventually found an airline agent who provided me with the clarity I needed—in English! Our plane had simply been diverted because of Hurricane Charley's arrival in south Florida. We would need to spend several hours in the airport, but she directed us to a place where we could buy some meals and relax until the flight was able to continue safely to Miami. When you travel with college athletes, you must feed them every couple of hours!

—

Have you ever felt overwhelmed and underresourced as a ministry leader? You want to lead well, but you just don't feel completely up to the task. Consider these statistics:

- Only one out of ten pastors will stay in vocational ministry until retirement.[1]
- Every month in the US alone, 1,700 people leave vocational ministry.[2]
- Within the next five years, 45 percent of nonprofit employees plan to find a job outside the nonprofit sector.[3]

The statistics themselves don't tell the whole story. God calls many pastors and ministers out of vocational ministry to build his kingdom in other ways, myself included. But I've spent years working with churches and nonprofit organizations, and I've known many leaders on the verge of quitting because they were exhausted and lacked the resources, internal and external, they needed. I know from experience that ministry leaders frequently find themselves in uncharted or unfamiliar territories just like I did in that Brazilian airport. They want to lead and love those they're called to serve. They have a heart to protect them and provide for them. But the challenges of leadership keep coming—limited resources, increasing demands, and social changes that complicate ministry.

If that's you, my heart aches for you. You don't just need a leadership pep talk. I've given more than my share of pep talks, but motivational speeches alone never won a game, regardless of what Hollywood tells you. The reason my players were successful is our pep talks flowed from a well-defined development program. To stay in the game, ministry leaders need more than inspiring quotes—they need new skills and refined leadership strategies.

—

Many years ago, I was privileged to speak at the Christian Alliance for Orphans annual conference. It's an amazing organization dedicated to seeing *every* child experience God's unfailing love. I was so touched, so humbled by the compassion I saw in the hearts of these men and women for vulnerable children throughout the world. To be candid, I wasn't just humbled; I was embarrassed. As a man who professed Christ as my Lord, I felt ashamed to be with these leaders who were living out their faith with an overwhelming passion that exceeded my own.

I began praying that God would break my heart like that, but I didn't know who "my people" were supposed to be. Driving late one night, I cried out, "Lord, who are my people? Who are my 'orphans'?" And then, in a moment I'll never forget, God gave me a powerful sense of clarity. "I've already given you a people to serve. I have given you leaders," the Holy Spirit seemed to say. "Shepherd the shepherds, teach the teachers, rescue the rescuers,

serve the servants, and encourage the encouragers. They are your
'orphans.' I have broken your heart for them.'"

I share my story with you because I'm called, heart and soul,
to serve leaders at all levels. Every godly leader wants to grow,
but few have a tangible, practical plan. This book is for the youth
pastor wanting to do more than play games and give weekly talks.
She's hungry to learn how to lead her students and team toward
Jesus. If that's you, this book will help you develop a personal,
lifelong leadership-growth strategy.

Or maybe you're a leader who feels the way I did in that
Brazilian airport—overwhelmed, underresourced, and uncertain
of your next steps. If you're a pastor who loves the church but feels
unequal to the task of ministry leadership, you might be focused
on the apostle Peter's words to pastors:

> Be shepherds of God's flock that is under your
> care, watching over them—not because you must,
> but because you are willing, as God wants you
> to be; not pursuing dishonest gain, but eager to
> serve; not lording it over those entrusted to you,
> but being examples to the flock. (1 Peter 5:2–3)

If you are watching over your flock willingly and trying to
be an example, but you've never been taught how to lead without
lording over those you serve, this book is for you. If you're trying
to break free from a conflict-avoidant posture in leadership, I
wrote this book for you too.

As I wrote, I thought about the thousands of men and women
who lead high-impact nonprofits in our cities, lay leaders trying to
hold a pastorless church together, and thousands of home church
pastors around the world.

If you're a ministry leader who wants to love and serve your
people, to protect and provide for them, and to build the kingdom
of God together with your team, *The Five-Day Leader* will be your

insanely practical guide to relentless growth, ridiculous routines, and resilient relationships.

What Is Leadership?

At its core, leadership is the ability to influence others. It's estimated that the typical human influences at least eighty thousand people throughout their lifetime.[4] Talk about a platform! And we all have one. All of us. Yes, some have larger platforms than others. My friends John and Lisa Bevere are international speakers, authors, and ministry founders who reach multitudes through their books, courses, and social media. But they also have small platforms—around the kitchen table with their family, at the golf course with people they just met, in an airport when they travel, and in their own neighborhood. Every one of us interacts with thousands of people throughout our lives, and every interaction is an opportunity for influence.

> *Every interaction is an opportunity for influence.*

So the question isn't *if* we'll influence others but if we'll influence them in *the right ways, toward the right things.* I remember the first time I felt the frightening responsibility of being a leader. Fresh out of college, I was a first-year teacher and coach. Just a few weeks in, I realized the students were actually listening to me. During lunch duty (new teachers always got lunch duty), they would hang around me and ask questions. As a coach, I'd invite players to my home to watch games, and *all* of them would show up. I had the sobering realization that these young people were influenced by my teaching, encouraged by my words, and modeling my behaviors.

Maybe you felt that same apprehension when you preached your first message, when you were given a leadership position that would push you to your limits, or when they handed you your newborn child. It's overwhelming, isn't it?

This book is driven by the belief that leadership isn't a special gift for a select few, but a behavior or practice that anyone can strengthen. Equipping and encouraging ministry leaders is my mission in life. By God's grace, I've been a college basketball coach, a church planter, a public educator, a business leader, and the executive senior pastor of one of the largest churches in America. I speak to nationally known corporations, nonprofits, and churches about leadership. I once even coached an astronaut, so I like to say that my influence is "out of this world" (even as my wife, Ronda, rolls her eyes).

I've worked with some of the most influential leaders of our generation, studied leadership from every angle, and discovered the behaviors that all great leaders share. Through these experiences the most important lesson that I have learned is this: *you* can become a better leader. No exceptions. The secret is simple enough: intentionality. Intentionality brings increase.

> *Intentionality brings increase.*

I need to clarify something else before we continue. This is *not* a self-help book. I make this vital distinction for two reasons.

First, personal growth isn't just personal. Growing is never just for our own benefit. As it says in 1 Peter 4:10: "Each of you should use whatever gift you have received to serve others, as faithful stewards of God's grace in its various forms." Using your God-given gifts to serve others isn't optional; it's the very reason they were given to you. We should be compelled to grow our ability to lead and influence others to serve them better. You are responsible for the resources and relationships God has placed in front of you.

> *You are responsible for the resources and relationships God has placed in front of you.*

Second, we can't ever *really* help ourselves. Think again about all the ways in which you feel overwhelmed and underresourced, then read the apostle Paul's words:

> We do not want you to be uninformed, brothers and sisters, about the troubles we experienced in the province of Asia. We were under great pressure, far beyond our ability to endure, so that we despaired of life itself. Indeed, we felt we had received the sentence of death. *But this happened that we might not rely on ourselves but on God*, who raises the dead. (2 Corinthians 1:8–9, emphasis added)

I have often felt out of my depth as a leader, and each of those times were an opportunity to press into God and rely more on him. As you read this book, you may occasionally feel *more* overwhelmed. It's my prayer that those moments will push you to rely on God and not yourself.

———

The purpose of this book is to provide you with a straightforward roadmap to intentionally grow as a leader with the Holy Spirit's help. We may not be able to *self-help*, but we can certainly *self-hinder* what God wants to do in our life. Relying on the Holy Spirit doesn't remove our responsibility to do the sort of things that allow growth. Over my past several decades leading and coaching leaders, I've discovered and distilled processes that steward our God-given strengths while addressing our personal limitations. It's been my privilege to work with leaders who were both humble and motivated, including:

- Anna, a survivor of human trafficking who founded a nonprofit to free and restore others like herself. She needed help scaling her organization as its growth outpaced her leadership experience.
- Dan, the new pastor of a church that had been rocked by a scandal. He needed tools to restore trust and heal a broken team.
- Tanya, whose nonprofit was on the front lines of lifting people out of inner-city poverty. She'd been left discouraged and disillusioned by the perpetual lack of resources and volunteers.

My goal is to walk you through the same kind of process I used with Anna, Dan, and Tanya. Here's the game plan: I'll start by unveiling five crippling leadership myths, giving you the "five-minute definition" of leadership and showing you the five things people need from their leaders. Next, I'll teach you the "3Rs of Leadership": relentless growth, ridiculous routines, and resilient relationships. Finally, I'll walk you through the Five-Day Plan, which will give you three action items for each weekday.

To be clear, *The Five-Day Leader* isn't a five-day program that will magically turn you into a leader. I'm a runner—even when I'm not being chased—and I can tell you that a single three-mile run will not change your life. But if you start *consistently* running three miles every other day, you'll have more energy, your health and quality of life will improve, and your newly found discipline will ripple into every area. It will change your life.

That's the idea behind *The Five-Day Leader.* Do it for one

week and you might feel a little different, but intentionally create a new set of habits—each specifically matched to one of the five days of the workweek—and this straightforward system will help you become a better steward of the relationships and influence Christ has entrusted to you. I've even created some free resources you can download here: www.the5dayleader.com.

That's it, simple and direct. I frequently tell my teammates and those we serve, "Don't make an easy thing hard." I promise not to overcomplicate things but instead to teach this process in a way that is powerful, practical, and life changing.

FIVE CRIPPLING MYTHS

Leadership is big business. Literally billions of dollars are spent on books, podcasting, workshops, and coaching. I'm in that business, so it'd be disingenuous to attack it. I'm honestly grateful for all the valuable resources out there. But just like all the competing, and sometimes contradictory, dieting advice available to anyone looking for it, a lot of leadership training is ineffective and can even be harmful and un-Christlike.

My job isn't correcting every leadership myth on the internet or in print. But I want to clear away five specific ones that may be hiding in your heart and preventing you from fully embracing your role as a ministry leader.

Myth #1: Leadership is a title.

This belief is two myths in one. On one hand, most people think that if they don't have an official role or title, they aren't really a leader. That's nonsense. I've known many churches where a staff member, even an administrative assistant, had more influence (and power) than the senior pastor. I've worked with thousands of organizations, and rarely is the most influential person the one listed at the top of the organizational chart. Very rarely. Leadership is influence, not a title. And yearning for a title is frequently no more than vanity.

On the other hand, immature leaders think that leadership starts—and stops—with having a title or a slot on the org chart. Protocol may require a master chief petty officer to salute a lower-ranked, newly commissioned ensign, but if that junior officer tries to boss the master chief around, he'll quickly learn about rank versus authority. On occasion a leader needs to "pull rank" (usually in a time of crisis) but *relying* on positional authority demonstrates a lack of influence.

As I said, it's the rare organization where the person at the top of the org chart is also the most influential. Those organizations are exceptional—in both senses of the word. Their leaders can marshal and inspire their people through influence while directing the organization's resources through title, thereby achieving extraordinary goals. So don't make the mistake of belittling or avoiding positional authority but do make building influence your focus. Together, they open great doors.

Myth #2: Leadership is complex.

Those familiar with the Bible know it's simple enough for children to understand while also being so complex scholars have been analyzing and interpreting it for centuries. Leadership is similar. You can study and practice leadership skills for decades but still have a lot to learn. Yet even a preschooler is capable of leading other preschoolers.

The core of leadership is *the ability to influence people*, nothing more. Some ways of leading are better and some are worse. I'll teach you some better ways, but you can lead right now with what you already know. Strike that. You already are leading and influencing others, so why not improve your ability to influence?

> *Leadership is the ability to influence people.*

I love basketball. A lot of people say that, but how many named their kids Michael and Jordan? I've played it since I was five and started coaching when I was nineteen, first at a middle school and finally as a head coach at the collegiate level. I love how accessible this sport is. All you need is a ball and a hoop, and the fundamentals are easy to teach. You can hand a ball to a toddler and say, "Throw this into that hoop." Building on the foundation of simple fundamentals, many athletes have developed championship-winning skills. Likewise, by teaching simple leadership skills, my aim is to see your influence increase to extraordinary levels. So think of this book as me tossing you a basketball. You're going to learn a lot more than shooting a free throw, but it starts with a pass and a catch.

Myth #3: Leadership is personality type.

Are leaders introverts or extroverts? Which Myers-Briggs type are they? What's their Enneagram number? The correct answers are "yes," "any," and "any." Think of all the people who have influenced you—family members, teachers, bosses, pastors—and you'll probably notice they represent just about every personality type. Your experience confirms that leadership isn't limited to specific personality types, but it's easy to subconsciously have a certain mental picture of a leader. Rip that picture off the wall, and throw it in the trash. Replace it with your favorite selfie. That's what a leader looks like.

I'm not saying your personality is irrelevant. The type of person you are will define *how* you lead. I don't want to dive into personality theory here, but here's a useful paradigm.

When something happens to you, you think something about

it a certain way, you feel a certain way, and you act in a certain way. Think, feel, and act. Those are the three universal responses. Everyone does all three. What changes from person to person is which one they do *first*. You see these three personalities in the early church:

- *Peter acted first.* From jumping out of a boat in the middle of a lake to chopping off an ear or denying Jesus, he acted first and thought second.
- *Paul thought first.* When he discovered his beloved church in Galatia was going off the rails, he wrote a theological treatise.
- *John felt first.* He was "the disciple Jesus loved" and was entrusted with Jesus's mother, and he was the one who filled his epistles with words of love.

Notice that God used, and still uses, every type of leader to build his kingdom. Which one are you: an act-first, think-first, or feel-first person? I'm an act-first leader, which is great in a crisis but has resulted in some less-than-stellar dad moments. The time my seventeen-year-old daughter broke her left thumb in a basketball game comes to mind. The school's athletic trainer suggested we take her to the hospital, and I said, "She's right-handed. Get her back on the court and we can go to the hospital after the game!" *Ouch.* We are all works in progress, my friend. Thank God for his grace to me (and my family).

Different types of leaders may thrive in different situations, so never compare yourself to another leader. Whichever type you are, remember that God uses every type of leader to build his kingdom. Each of us, regardless of personality type, can take responsibility for ourselves and learn the behaviors that increase influence and gain credibility.

> *God uses every type of leader to build his kingdom.*

Myth #4: Leadership is for a select few.

Some so-called leadership experts promote the idea that only an elite cross section of any population has natural leadership ability—a privileged few with the charisma, skill, and calling to lead. Even when you know that's nonsense, you may still feel unqualified to be a ministry leader.

However, in the Sermon on the Mount, Jesus said, "Let your light shine before others, that they may see your good deeds and glorify your Father in heaven" (Matthew 5:16). This is a universal call to influence others, and influence is leadership. Therefore, leadership is a universal calling.

Our presence is never neutral. Whenever we connect with an individual, our family, a team at work, or a group in our church or community, we move their needle in a positive or negative direction. Understanding and embracing that reality is a significant step toward taking responsibility for our own behavior and the impact we have on others. Maybe the reason we believe this myth is to avoid that responsibility.

Myth #5: Leadership growth occurs in significant moments.

We've all seen movies where the protagonist refuses to accept his or her responsibility/calling/destiny, but just when all hope seems lost, some event/mentor/memory changes everything, and the hero saves the day. But that's rarely how life works. The classic movie *Dead Poets Society*[1] is more realistic. Mr. Keating influenced his students over the course of months, not with a single rousing speech.

Certainly, the class experienced significant moments, as when one of the students climbed up on his desk and declared, "O Captain! My Captain!" But those are almost always the culmination of countless seemingly insignificant moments. As a husband, I remember a few crucial events that helped define our marriage, but the real credit for our thirty years together goes to the simple behaviors that my wife and I practiced over time. It's those little ways we choose to "value others above yourselves" (Philippians 2:3), such as me walking Ronda to her car every morning when she leaves for work, and her always putting a blanket on me when I doze off watching a game. In the same way, we as parents had a few "stake in the ground" conversations with our children, but our influence predominately came from small, daily actions—like our "debriefing conversations" on the way home from school, cleaning the kitchen together, and bedtime routines.

Influencing others is a moment-to-moment endeavor that creates a lifelong and eternal impact. This understanding requires three specific mindsets:

1. Don't waste your time looking for some magic trick to become a better leader. Waiting for a singular transformational moment makes as much sense as a retirement strategy based on winning the lottery.

2. Don't get discouraged by your mistakes. Michael Jordan missed more than nine thousand shots and lost almost three hundred games. The secret to success is to persist through the failures, learn from the mistakes, and embrace growth. Great leadership is a process of putting influential moments together, each day, through many seasons of life.

3. Similarly, be patient with the people you're leading. As a coach, I noticed that the lessons that didn't seem to get through to a freshman often showed up by the time he was a junior. Likewise, parents know that "Wash your

hands after using the bathroom" and "Eat your veggies" aren't one-time lessons. Influencing others is a long-term process. Don't give up when your inspirational speech fails to revolutionize your team. Fruit takes time to grow.

———

I can refute every one of these myths with this one statement: Leadership isn't just an attitude (though attitude is key); leadership is an action. That's what we're going to talk about in the next chapter.

Reflection: Take a moment and reflect on each of these myths. If you could magically erase one of them from your mind to create the greatest impact on your leadership, which one would you choose?

CHAPTER 3

FIVE-MINUTE
DEFINITION

"A great concept can be explained in five minutes but discussed for five days."

I don't remember where I heard that, but it stuck with me. Anyone who knows me will tell you I'm all about efficiency. I love not having to wade through a three-hundred-page book for a couple of life-changing ideas. Remember my rule—don't make an easy thing hard.

So start the clock. Here's my five-minute definition of leadership: Leadership is a behavior that influences others and drives outcomes.

> *Leadership is a behavior that influences others and drives outcomes.*

Since that only took a few seconds, I'll use the rest of my time explaining the three key points of that definition.

1. Leadership is a behavior.

Leadership isn't defined by a title or a position but by behavior. Isn't that like saying, "Love is a behavior"? Isn't leadership about attitude, knowledge, and skill? Yes, but all those things are internal and, therefore, invisible. Leadership, like love, will ultimately be seen only through its actions. You can't say you love someone if you don't act lovingly; you can't call yourself a leader if you don't act like one.

This is really good news for you. Why? Because *leadership behaviors can be learned, practiced, and improved*. No one is born with all the leadership tools they need, but everyone can study, develop, and put those tools into action. Again, attitude and knowledge *contribute* to your ability to lead, but ultimately, what you do and the way you do it is what will create credibility and the ability to influence others.

> *Leadership behaviors can be learned, practiced, and improved.*

Leadership is like love in another way. We must behave like leaders even if we're not feeling it at the moment. Love is intended to be unconditional, regardless of circumstances. In the same way, we must take responsibility for our leadership *behaviors*, committing to lead well, even in difficult situations. Even when we are tired, confused, frustrated, or angry. In fact, those are the moments when we really learn to rely not on ourselves but on God.

2. Leadership is about others.

Leadership behaviors *can* be used to influence others to get what we want. That's manipulation, pure and simple. Christlike leadership, however, is always for the benefit others. Whether you're leading a home church, a megachurch, a nonprofit ministry, home group, or youth group, your ultimate example is Jesus, who said:

> I am the good shepherd. The good shepherd lays down his life for the sheep. The hired hand is not the shepherd and does not own the sheep. So when he sees the wolf coming, he abandons the sheep and runs away. Then the wolf attacks the flock and scatters it. The man runs away because he is a hired hand and cares nothing for the sheep. (John 10:11–14)

Too many so-called leaders are in it for themselves. Never mind what they say, their behavior proves they're about building their own empire, not caring for others. That's worse than being a hired hand. It's being a wolf that devours the sheep he's supposed to lead. I could write a book about that (and someday probably will). If your leadership isn't about others, it's broken.

> *If leadership isn't about others, it's broken.*

One of my favorite biblical examples of others-focused leadership is from the Old Testament, when the Lord said to Moses, "Look at the land with your own eyes, since you are not going to cross this Jordan. But commission Joshua, and *encourage and strengthen him*, for he will lead this people across and will cause them to inherit the land that you will see" (Deuteronomy 3:27–28, emphasis added). One challenging but illuminating test of biblical leadership is the ability to rejoice when others "inherit the land," even without you. That requires trusting God to take care of your needs and setting aside your personal agenda and taking up the success of others.

3. Leadership is about results.

I have been both a playground monitor and a championship basketball coach, and while you might think those positions are equally about overseeing a group of young people as they play, they're actually quite different. The monitor's job is simply to keep all the kids safe and playing nice (which can be tough enough!). But a coach organizes and unites a group of individuals, inspires them, and trains them to play a game. Because their desired outcomes are different, the leadership required of the positions is different. Leadership roles are defined and differentiated by their desired outcomes.

The key word here is *outcome*. Many times, on a beautiful December day in south Florida, the last thing my players *wanted* to do was practice for two hours, put up five hundred extra shots following practice, and then lift weights for an hour. But their desired outcome was to become better basketball players, so I taught and trained them in a manner that would lead to success. I served them by ignoring their immediate desire (to join others at the beach) in favor of their long-term goal (to become champions).

Results-focused leadership requires leading with a specific destination in mind. That destination varies greatly according to the situation, but I believe it comes down to one word, a word that's going to be incredibly helpful throughout our journey: *better*. Our role as leaders is to influence people to become better. Better people, better Christ-followers, better employees, better students, better parents, better spouses, and better friends. Not perfect, but better. We want to give them better tools to achieve desired outcomes, better teaching to avoid mistakes, and better encouragement to inspire better goals.

Like the servants in Jesus's parable of the talents (Matthew 25:14–30), leaders are always a steward of someone else's authority and resources. Even if you don't report to a board or donors, you're still responsible to God for your actions and your team's outcomes.

Sometimes this responsibility requires buckling down on a teenager who's texting friends instead of watching the kids they're babysitting or introducing consequences to team members who continue to do substandard work. Even then, you are still required to direct others toward the desired outcomes. How? By focusing on their deeper needs, such as learning responsibility. By working with them at the first signs of a problem instead of avoiding conflict. By doing whatever it takes to help them get better.

—

I love the original *Top Gun*[1] movie. Tom Cruise's character, Maverick, is true to his name. All he cares about is proving himself at any cost, and he blows it off when Iceman calls him dangerous. It isn't until his selfish ambition leads to his best friend's death that he finally recognizes that his attitude and actions were dangerous and accepts the responsibility to protect others. While most of us aren't in literal life-and-death situations, self-serving leadership focused on power and ego can be just as dangerous to those entrusted to our care.

In the next chapter, we're going to look at five things people need from their leaders, but first I'd like you to take a moment to examine your motives. Why do you want to become a better leader? Do you want to serve others better or to get better at making them serve you?

You've probably read this passage a hundred times, but I want you to read it once more, this time as God's instruction manual for leadership:

> Do nothing out of selfish ambition or vain conceit.
> Rather, in humility value others above yourselves,
> not looking to your own interests but each of you

to the interests of the others. In your relationships with one another, have the same mindset as Christ Jesus: Who, being in very nature God, did not consider equality with God something to be used to his own advantage; rather, he made himself nothing by taking the very nature of a servant, being made in human likeness. And being found in appearance as a man, he humbled himself by becoming obedient to death—even death on a cross! (Philippians 2:3–8)

Many unrecognized leaders serve others with Christlike humility, while some of the most well-known leaders leave destruction in their wake. Some of my deepest regrets come from the way I treated others when I was selfish and pushed for my agenda, my comfort, and my desires. Acknowledging my failures brings me to a place of humility, where I ask God for forgiveness and the grace to become a better leader tomorrow than I am today.

Reflection: Take a moment to reread and reflect on this passage. Do you need to repent of your pride, self-interest, or selfish ambition?

CHAPTER

PEOPLE NEED LEADERS

I n the last chapter, I defined leadership as a behavior that influences others and drives outcomes. Marcus Buckingham, in his book *The One Thing You Need to Know,* says it this way: "Great leaders rally people to a better future."[1]

He goes on to discuss anthropologist Donald Brown's research on "human universals"—372 features, from baby talk to fear of snakes to music, which can be found in all societies. Buckingham boils these down into five universal fears that raise anxiety in every human being on the planet: death, isolation, the future, chaos, and insignificance.[2] This may be controversial and defy some modern beliefs of our individualistic society, but I believe these five fears demonstrate our universal *need* for leadership. Each of the five fears represent a corresponding need we, as leaders, should address. God gives us leaders to help us overcome fear and provide for our needs.

Our role as leaders is to serve others, remember. If our leadership isn't about others, then it is broken. As we engage with and influence others, our responsibility is to address their fears and, more importantly, meet their needs. This may feel overwhelming, and you may not feel up to the task. That is because you aren't up to the task. Neither am I. Once again, we are forced to rely on God's grace. Grace doesn't just mean having your sins forgiven. It also means that God steps in and makes up the massive gap between what is required of you and what you can do. Sometimes that means he gives you abilities beyond your resources. Sometimes that simply means that he meets those needs in our place. However, his grace doesn't absolve us of our responsibility to care for and connect with those he has called us to influence. Let's take a look at the way leaders can meet people's basic needs.

1. Fear of Death—The Need for Security

Your job as a leader is to protect those you lead. Pastors protect their congregations from false teachers and warn about sin's destructiveness. Nonprofit leaders mobilize resources to provide for the helpless. Board members protect the organization against abusive leaders. Leaders who fail to protect their most vulnerable people or, worse yet, are the ones inflicting the harm are under God's judgment. We all have seen the news stories about organizations that have protected popular leaders instead of the victims of their abuse. This is without excuse.

Please remember that security means more than physical protection. Our responsibilities as leaders mean we preserve the social and emotional security of those we influence as well. Do you have a temper? All of us do—some just have a shorter fuse. But when we express our anger in unhealthy ways at our team, their anxiety goes up, and rather than improve their performance, anxiety frequently has a negative impact on performance. So yelling may get people to move faster, but in the long term they'll perform worse.

Are you a harsh critic, one of those leaders who is hard, if not impossible, to please? We all believe in high standards, but the way we offer our critique and when we choose to share it can have a significant impact on the social and emotional security of others. When I was coaching basketball, my goal was to praise and encourage in a volume that everyone in the arena could hear but critique and correct in a way that only the individual player I was addressing would hear.

2. Fear of Isolation—The Need for Community

Everyone's looking for belonging. We all have the need to be a part of something bigger than ourselves and to feel like we belong. "It is not good for man to be alone" doesn't just apply to marriage. It's a truth that resonates for all people and all the relationships we have. Remember this: human beings are like herd animals. We naturally look for reasons to connect. I travel all over the world coaching leaders, and whenever I meet someone, the conversation usually goes something like this:

"Where are you from?" they ask.

"College Station, Texas," I say.

"Where's that?"

"About ninety minutes northwest of Houston."

"Oh! My aunt lives in Houston. Maybe you know her."

About seven million people live in Houston, so I don't like those odds. But what do you think is really happening here? This person is trying to connect with me.

The need for community is universal. This means all people will find a community to connect to and be influenced by. As ministry leaders, we want people to connect in a healthy, life-giving way. And you'll know when the need for community is not being met—you'll see relationships filled with sarcasm, passive-aggressive behavior, defiance, and cynicism.

If everyone you serve has a need for community, part of your role as a ministry leader is to develop healthy connections with the people you lead. Keep in mind, these community-building relationships can't be one-sided. Your people need *you* to be relational. "I'm not a people person" isn't a legitimate excuse.

You must connect with your people in meaningful, consistent, and intentional ways. If you are unwilling to do so, you need to repent. If you are unable to do so, you need to figure out why not.

3. Fear of the Future—The Need for Clarity

A minute ago, I talked about how anxiety inhibits performance. Do you know the antidote to anxiety? Clarity. If rumors of bankruptcy circulate around your office, what happens? Anxiety goes up. But if the boss clearly communicates the full story, what to expect, and what everyone needs to do, anxiety goes down as employees regain a sense of understanding and, therefore, control. They still can't solve the company's financial problems, but they can make a plan for their individual response to what's likely to happen.

In C. S. Lewis's novel *That Hideous Strength*,[3] the demonic director dominates his staff through vague and shifting expectations. This leaves the staff paralyzed with fear, full of frustration, and with a constant feeling of failure. Lewis's novel is an excellent illustration of what happens when a leader refuses to meet his people's need for security. As children of the light, we serve our teams through clear expectations, honest assessments, and transparent communication.

The most effective teams and leaders that I work with have clarity regarding their mission, clarity of how each person on the team is connected to the mission, and clarity of responsibilities they must execute to fulfill the mission.

There's also a deeper clarity that Christian leaders can provide to their people. We can replace fear of the future with *hope*. Hope is more than a "the glass is half full" optimism. It is the foundational belief that "in all things God works for the good of those who love him, who have been called according to his purpose" (Romans 8:28). This doesn't mean everything *is* good, but that God is directing everything toward a good outcome. This creates a clear-sighted hope in the face of even the greatest trials.

4. Fear of Chaos—The Need for Authority

The Hebrew word *shalom*, usually translated "peace," is far bigger than tranquility. In the ancient Near East worldview, chaos was the greatest threat, and their creation stories were all about the gods wrestling order out of the chaos. But in Genesis, God simply speaks to the formless void (Genesis 1:2) and creates order, beauty, and well-being—shalom. When he tells Adam to "fill the earth and subdue it" (Genesis 1:28), God is basically saying, "Bring my shalom to the world on my behalf." This is still our job as Christians—bringing God's shalom to a world in moral, spiritual, and physical chaos.

Chaos is a luxury that leaders cannot afford. Even if they can function well in a disorganized system, most of their people cannot. Well-run organizations accomplish more because their employees can focus their energy on their duties instead of surviving the chaos. And they can do so because they have confidence in their leaders to not just manage that chaos but protect them from it. One of the best things we can do as ministry leaders is bring clarity where there is chaos, whether in our personal lives or on our teams. Much of that can be done by focusing on working through our personal issues and on a team level, clarifying our mission.

Recently while I traveled to an event, my initial flight was delayed, resulting in a tight connection to my second flight. Compounding my angst was the fact that my connecting airport was one that I rarely flew through and wasn't even a little familiar with. As my plane landed, the lack of clarity about my next steps and the chaos of people pushing their way off the plane cranked up my anxiety to an extreme level. Suddenly, a young man who must have overheard my conversation with the flight attendant regarding the situation asked me where my connecting gate was. When I told him, he gave me the troubling news that it was located a significant walk and tram ride away from our arrival gate. Sensing my anxiety, he smiled and said, "I got you. We'll get to your flight together."

This stranger and I stepped off the plane and broke into a jog. With efficiency (I never looked at one sign, keeping my eyes on him instead) and effectiveness (we made the trip through a busy airport in less than seven minutes), he helped me reach my flight. Just like that, a young man I'd never met and may never see again gave me a beautiful illustration of leadership. He was willing to surrender a portion of his time (leadership isn't about us; it's about others), and he used his knowledge and experience (he knew this airport extremely well) to influence me (reduce my anxiety) and help me achieve my desired outcome (make it to my next flight on time).

I am an experienced traveler and certainly capable of reading signs and following arrows, but in that moment of anxiety I was so thankful for that young man and his willingness to be a difference-maker in my life. Sometimes the people we are leading need to hear what I heard that day: "I got you. I will walk with you." They simply need us to use our authority to cut through the chaos and take care of them.

Keep in mind, leading people through chaos and serving well can often mean focusing on someone who needs extra attention. I want to encourage you to leave the ninety-nine to care for the one. But remember, when Christ left the ninety-nine, he did not leave them hanging. He left them safely on the hill while he searched for the one lost sheep (Matthew 18:12–14). While we serve, we need to listen to the Holy Spirit to be able to care for everyone we lead.

5. Fear of Insignificance—The Need for Respect

I grew up the only child of a widowed mother. She was one of the most amazing leaders I will ever know, and her influence developed my work ethic, my love to read and learn, and my capacity to care for others. She was a fifth-grade teacher, so we'd arrive at school an hour and a half early every morning. As Mom would prepare her lessons and set up her room, I'd entertain myself in the gym. Basketball became my sport because it's the only sport you can play alone, but with the vivid imagination that only children are known for, that empty gym was transformed every morning. In my mind, I played against Magic Johnson or Larry Bird in Madison Square Garden, filled with twenty thousand screaming fans. It was the final game of the NBA finals, and we were down by two with one second left on the clock. I raced down the court and fired off a three-pointer to win the game.

I played hundreds of imaginary games, but do you know the one thing I never did? Pass the ball to one of my fictional teammates so he could make the winning shot. No, I was always the hero. That's the point. No one wants to be average. Everyone wants to be the hero.

> *No one wants to be average.*

I believe meeting this need for significance is the responsibility and privilege of the leader—we get to help *others* be the hero, to be more than average. I have heard this called this the Cinderella principle of leadership—everyone wants a fairy godmother to take them from where they're currently stuck to where they want to go. I am not implying that everyone wants to be a senior pastor, CEO, or professional athlete. Rather, I'm saying that dignity matters to each of us, and we desire to pursue opportunities and perform at a level where we can experience a high degree of self-respect as well as earn the respect of others.

As I mentioned earlier, I'm a runner, although not a very fast one. I enjoy running races, and every time I do, I am reminded of our universal need for respect. Many of the races I run have thousands of participants—some there to compete and win, some there to attempt a personal best time, and many there simply to challenge themselves and receive a sense of accomplishment. The beauty of this process is that everyone who crosses the finish line on race day, regardless of their time, does so with a tremendous sense of dignity—and a crowd is always there cheering to acknowledge that.

Everyone we lead is running a race of some sort. As their leaders it is our joy and privilege to equip them, encourage them, acknowledge them, and ultimately dignify them.

—

I could say a lot more about what leadership is and isn't, but I promised not to overcomplicate things. It's time to move on to the work of becoming a better leader. And buckle up because it's going to involve change. After all, doing things the way you've always done them won't work. We have a saying down here in Texas: if nothing changes, then nothing changes.

For example, I am writing this chapter early in the morning in a hotel room. I've been shivering for the last fifteen minutes, but because I want to finish this chapter before taking a break to turn up the thermostat and put on a sweatshirt, I continue to shiver. Out of my stubborn nature, I'm refusing to do anything different—and unsurprisingly, I'm still cold. This is the way many leaders are living their lives. The results of their current behaviors are not ideal, but they remain in that condition because they're unwilling to alter their behavior.

Embrace this truth as we begin this journey: if you want to empower people to create a better future, you must commit to intentionally developing your leadership skills and engaging in new behaviors that result in better outcomes for you and your people.

I've worked with leaders meeting the needs of their people in every possible domain: business, professional and college athletics, education, military, and ministry. By studying their behaviors, I've identified three characteristics that all highly effective leaders have in common. I call these my "3Rs of Leadership":

1. Having a relentless commitment to growth
2. Practicing ridiculous routines
3. Building lasting, resilient relationships

Just three things, none of them too complex and none of them outside of your capacity to develop. You're probably already doing them on some level.

If you stick with me through the 5-Day Leader process, you'll learn to intentionally integrate the 3Rs into your daily life and revolutionize your leadership. They've changed my life, and I believe they'll change yours. Let's press on.

RELENTLESS GROWTH

As a college basketball coach, one of my favorite times of the year was when our players came back to campus in the fall. Both the new year and the new team were full of possibilities. Before our first practice, I'd gather the team together and ask this reflection question: "If 'now you' were to play one-on-one with 'last-year you,' who would win, and why?" Of course, my guys would say "now me" and talk about how much more experience they had, the thousands of shots they have taken in practice, and the countless conditioning sessions that enhanced their strength and stamina.

But what if I had changed the question to "end-of-season you" versus "end-of-summer you"? That would probably be a different story. I had my players' statistics from the previous year, and by the time our first practice was over I could tell who had coasted and who had practiced diligently over the summer.

Basketball is not like riding a bicycle. Your body quickly atrophies, and muscle memory gets fuzzy. Just maintaining your current abilities requires significant effort. Unless you're actively getting better, you're passively getting worse.

> *Unless you're actively getting better,*
> *you're passively getting worse.*

Add to that the increasing expectations as you progress. What dazzled folks back in high school is the bare minimum in college. And what impressed me as a college coach would barely earn you a look from NBA scouts.

The same is true of leadership. The skills that got you the promotion are likely not enough to make you thrive in your new role. As you're entrusted with greater leadership roles, you need to work all the harder to simply keep up with new challenges and expectations.

The most influential leaders I know are committed to growth. Not just a read an occasional book and go to a seminar or two type of growth, but *relentless* growth—intentionally and aggressively pursuing new skills and strategies, then applying them so they can better influence the people they care so deeply about. The reason they're high-level leaders isn't because of a special calling but because of their uncommon commitment to growth. If it weren't for that, they would still be struggling to gain the credibility and grow the influence they need to create positive outcomes.

This is my definition of *relentless growth*: "a passionate commitment to consistently add knowledge, skills, and perspective." Leaders with this mindset are unstoppable.

> *Relentless growth is "a passionate commitment to*
> *consistently add knowledge, skills, and perspective."*

Have you ever served under a leader who refused to grow? Been taught by a teacher whose syllabus was an nth generation photocopy? Worked for a boss who refused to listen to new ideas?

If so, you know the frustration of knowing how much more your team could do if that leader wasn't so lazy. But ask yourself, was laziness the real problem? Laziness may be the issue for some, but my experience is that most leaders work hard. Looking at my own life and the times that I've stalled or stopped my own growth journey, the issue wasn't laziness but a lack of intentionality and courage.

1. Lack of Intentionality

I have never said, "Growth isn't important." But as life got busy, the urgent shoved the truly important out of the way. I'd pick up a random book in the airport, listen to an occasional podcast, or have infrequent conversations with my mentors and coaches. But I lost my focus, my intentionality—and, therefore, the trajectory of my growth absolutely relented.

We have all participated in what I call "random acts of improvement." We exercise one day but then return to complacency the rest of the week. I might eat a healthy, green salad for lunch but then follow up with a dinner of queso, fajitas, and Dr Pepper. Random acts are positive behaviors, but without sustainability they never create the lasting impact we desire.

One of my teammates likes to remind us—constantly—that "greatness demands intentionality." Earlier I said that intentionality brings increase, meaning that what we focus on will always bear fruit, good or bad. As Christians who believe God has created us for a purpose, we are responsible to him for our continued growth and development. After all, just think of the ways your own life has benefited from others' intentional commitment to continued growth! I'm certainly grateful for teachers who kept learning so they could teach me more, doctors who kept up on medical advances to keep me healthy, and pastors who focused on their own growth so they could shepherd our church well.

> *Greatness demands intentionality.*

How do you maintain intentionality? That is literally the purpose of the 5-Day Leader process, so keep reading!

2. Lack of Courage

My dad was diagnosed with an aggressive cancer when my mom was pregnant with me and was near death in a hospital while I was being born a month prematurely at another hospital. When he heard that he had a son, he rallied and lived another six years to help raise me. When he died, he had tumors in every major organ. That's the kind of fight that I come from. "Wells do not quit" was the message pounded into my heart throughout my life. I was raised with extremely high expectations and expected to be the best in everything.

I'm incredibly grateful for this example and upbringing. It has made me the man I am. However, when my wife, Ronda, and I became parents, I set the bar for my children high—too high. I was relentless, and not always in a good way. I was all truth and no grace.

When my kids were still young, a dear truth-telling friend surprised me by saying, "Lyle, I think you're too hard on your children."

I was not expecting the confrontation, and everything in me wanted to argue with him, to defend and justify myself, and to even blame my parents. By God's grace, I listened, but I didn't really believe him.

That evening after the kids were in bed, I told Ronda what he'd said and asked what she thought. The look on her face cut me to my soul, and I was deeply convicted. In that moment, I made a commitment to change. I prayed for help and wisdom, I sought forgiveness from my wife and my children, and I began to change how I led my family. I thank God for that friend who was willing to confront me. I don't like to think about the damage I would have done to my children if I hadn't allowed God to change my heart.

Change is hard. Even getting out of bed on a cold day can take real effort. It's easier to stay under the covers, warm and content. Contentment means to be satisfied, which can be good or bad. We should be content in our status as justified, forgiven, and well-loved children of God. But we should never be content in our sanctification—the process of being shaped into the image of Christ and being filled with the fruit of the Spirit. That kind of contentment, and its next-door neighbor, complacency, are the enemies of growth.

At the time my friend confronted me, I was comfortable with my parenting. I was complacent. His simple statement made me angry, but that was just a cover for what I was really feeling: shame, fear, and hopelessness. At that moment, everything in me wanted to believe that he didn't know what he was talking about instead of facing the hard truth and doing the hard work required to grow. Choosing to listen to him, to talk to Ronda, and then take the steps necessary to change the way I parented were acts of courage.

The antidote to contentment and complacency is courage—courage to see the truth, to face your failures, and to do the hard work of change.

> *The antidote to contentment and complacency is courage.*

The Four Steps of Growth

1. Confrontation. I've discovered four key steps in the growth process. First is confrontation. Webster's dictionary says to confront means to "bring face-to-face" or to "encounter."[1]

Confrontation happens when God brings something specific to my attention, sometimes through an internal nudge and other times through someone else. He could use a loved one, a neighbor or coworker, or even a stranger at the grocery store or gym. Regardless of the source, confrontation is the moment I come face-to-face with a behavior that's hindering my ability to lead. It can be a sin I need to repent of or a behavior, character trait, or skill I need to develop. We see this happen in the story of Peter. As he denies Jesus and hears the rooster crowing, he remembers Jesus's words and comes face-to-face with the realization of his sin (Mark 14: 66–72). Another biblical example is God's use of Nathan, who opened David's eyes to his sin with both a parable and straightforward accusation of wrongdoing (2 Samuel 12:1–15).

Confrontation isn't always aggressive or adversarial. I can experience confrontation in a conversation with a friend when I realize that I am being stubborn or narrow-minded about an issue. I can be confronted with a challenge to grow by a sweet, short comment from Ronda or one of our kids about missing certain activities or not spending enough time together. Our team confronts each other in a loving, even fun, way when we practice "blameless problem solving"—dissecting an issue to make it, and us, better.

In one sense, confrontation is frequently our easiest step because it's often passive. It's done to us rather than us doing something, at least in the beginning. A mark of intentionality and relentless growth is actively welcoming healthy confrontation rather than shying away from it. That's a key feature of the 5-Day Leader process.

2. Conviction. The second step is conviction, and it's perhaps the hardest one. This is all about how you respond to the confrontation, and *that* will be the difference maker. Everything in you may want to justify or ignore the issue or, worse, attack the source. It's always easier to blame someone or something else than face your own failings. Will you do the hard thing instead and courageously accept the confrontation?

If I can go back to my preacher's roots for just a moment, I want to encourage you. It's much easier to embrace growth when you're secure in God's grace, love, and acceptance. It's easier to accept confrontation if your identity is rooted in being a child of God rather than what you do, because you understand that acknowledging a mistake or area of growth doesn't change your character or worth. Walking in humility always makes conviction easier to embrace. When I think about my worst moments as a leader, they always occurred when I wasn't walking in humility. Once I take my ego, or my identity, out of the equation, taking responsibility for my behaviors becomes possible, and conviction becomes the catalyst for a better version of my leadership.

3. Commitment. The third step is commitment. This is where you take concrete steps to respond to the conviction, and it's perhaps the most important step. If you regularly fail to act on conviction, the first two steps become *worse* than meaningless because you'll begin mistaking conviction for real change. In the commitment step, you pray, journal, read good books, and seek godly counsel and accountability. You create a game plan and keep track of your growth. Remember, you can't keep doing things the way you've always done them and expect to change—that's a road trip around the cul-de-sac of foolishness.

4. Change. Finally, the fourth step of true growth is experiencing change. This is the most rewarding step. As these new behaviors or lessons take root, you begin reaping the benefit of becoming a more Christlike Christ-follower and leader. Enjoy this part of your progress, but don't get content. Relentless growth means we remain vigilant for the next thing God will bring to mind that we need to confront.

Again, I want to emphasize that this isn't a self-help checklist. Every step is a gift of grace—even if it doesn't feel like it at the time. Being confronted is a gift from a God who loves us just the way we are but loves us too much to leave us there. Responding to the confrontation humbly requires grace. Identifying and accessing the resources we need for committing to change—and then following through—are a gift of grace. When we look back at each change that's occurred, we don't boast in ourselves but thank God for his grace.

—

Growth is its own reward and always pays off above and beyond what we put into it. Growth energizes us. Growth inspires us. Growth gives us confidence to take on new challenges in the future. It would be worth it even if we weren't leaders. But we are leaders, and relentless growth is a must. As I said in chapter 1, there is no such thing as purely "personal growth" for the leader. Your growth or stagnation as a leader leads to behaviors, skills, and attitudes that directly impact those you lead.

> *Your growth isn't personal—it directly impacts those you lead.*

Wise King Solomon wrote, "The complacency of fools will destroy them" (Proverbs 1:32). Complacency doesn't just destroy our credibility; it can destroy those we are called to serve. Again, think of how you've been negatively affected by leaders who refused to grow. We are responsible to the people we love and lead to relentlessly grow.

CHAPTER

RIDICULOUS ROUTINES

M y friend Mark, whom I've known since college, is a truly gifted leader who embodies the term "greatness demands intentionality" in a way that few ever have—and it shows up in both his professional and his personal life.

In his midtwenties, Mark decided he wanted to play a round of golf at every one of the nearly three hundred courses in his home state of Colorado, as well as play at least one round of golf in every other state. He recently turned sixty and has achieved both goals. How did he do it? Through ridiculous routines. Mark meticulously saved a little money from each paycheck for nearly forty years to fund his golf passion, and he scheduled time each spring break and every summer vacation to travel and play at these courses. Small investments of time and money over an extended period of nearly four decades helped make his dream come true.

Over those same decades, Mark also became one of the most successful and popular school superintendents in his state. He was highly regarded for his relationships with principals, teachers, students, and parents. One of the reasons, again, was his commitment to ridiculous routines. Throughout his career as a superintendent, Mark made a commitment to visit at least two campuses in his district every day. He also attended a minimum of three extracurricular events a week. These routines ensured he remained connected to the people he was leading so he could serve them well.

The Power of Routines

Routine is frequently viewed as something negative, indicating something boring or something that holds you back. Breaking out of the routine, therefore, is seen as brave, creative, and empowering. But depending on the routine, the opposite can be true. Stephen King and Jerry Seinfeld have both credited their enormous success to their routine of writing every day. Another example of the power of routines comes from professional sports. In professional football, basketball, and hockey, the home team wins about 65 percent of the time. Think about that. Statistically, they are almost twice as likely to win than the visiting team. Major League Baseball is different, though. Their home teams only have a 54 percent chance of winning. Why the difference? Are baseball fans less committed to their home team than other sports? No. It comes down to the power of routines. Let me explain.

Just like you and me, professional athletes have a limited amount of mental bandwidth. When they're playing on the road, little bits of that bandwidth go to a hundred little things that they don't normally have to think about—looking for a place to eat, adjusting to a new time zone, sleeping in an unfamiliar bed, orienting themselves to a new stadium. Any one of those things may not make a big difference by itself, but added together, they make a two-to-one difference.

Unlike football, basketball, and hockey teams that play their opposition just once in a week, baseball teams stay in a city for several days to play multiple games in a row. Having a string of consecutive nights in the same hotel and playing in the same stadium allow them to grow accustomed to a place—even developing routines for the week, thereby dramatically improving their performance.

The power of a routine comes from developing habits that become rhythms in your life, empowering you to grow your credibility and influence with others.

Choosing the Right Routines

From the couple who goes to the grocery store every Saturday morning with a stack of coupons in hand to my son-in-law, Seth, who thinks nothing of daily runs (even running twenty miles on a holiday), we all have routines that look ridiculous to outsiders. But some of those routines are more profitable than others.

A while back, I was working with a young CEO of a startup who was struggling to keep up with his responsibilities. He admitted to spending "too much" time playing video games.

"How much time?" I asked.

"Too much," he repeated, looking at the floor.

"How much?"

"I don't know. I don't like thinking about it."

"I need a number."

He did some math in his head, then said, "I guess around twenty to thirty." At first, I thought the number was minutes per day, so you can imagine my shock when he told me he meant twenty to thirty hours per week!

Thirty hours playing video games—almost a full-time job. That's a ridiculous routine.

In my study of high-level leaders, I found that they all had ridiculous routines. Like my friend Mark, they routinely connected with their people, dedicated time to learn and to grow, practiced discipline around self-care, and identified their priorities and remained focused on them. These routines demonstrate just as fanatical a commitment as playing video games thirty hours a week, but for something far more worthwhile.

Some outstanding examples of leaders with ridiculous routines include these:

- A company president takes one full day a month to sit in silence and solitude to think and dream about his organization.
- A colleague made a commitment to fitness more than twenty years ago with the mantra "sweat every day."
- One of my best friends blocks out two hours every Thursday afternoon to write notes of affirmation and encouragement to team members.
- A business leader comes into his office every Saturday morning for two hours to pray for each person in his company, every project they are currently working on, and every project in their pipeline.

If leadership is a behavior that influences others and drives outcomes, routines are where you create the patterns of behavior that develop those currencies. Ridiculous routines are repeatable behaviors that align with our priorities and accelerate our growth and impact on others.

> *Ridiculous routines are repeatable behaviors that align with our priorities and accelerate our growth and impact on others.*

That young CEO wasn't able to keep up with his own responsibilities, let alone have a positive impact on others, until he gave up his gaming habit. For you to become an effective leader, you'll have to give up some less beneficial routines and replace them with better ones, which comes down to priorities.

It's All about Priorities

Take a moment to carefully and prayerfully define your top five priorities. These are the things you value most and care about above all others. List them here:

1.
2.
3.
4.
5.

Now think through your routines, from how you spend your mornings to when you go to bed. What are the things you do every day or every week? List your five most ingrained habits here:

1.
2.
3.
4.
5.

Notice that your routines have been created one of two ways: (1) intentionally, as a reflection of your priorities (such as reading your Bible before your kids get up), or (2) unintentionally, as you slipped into a rut without resistance (such as mindlessly thumbing through your social media feed before falling asleep).

Here's what you must understand: whether your routines were created intentionally or unintentionally, they become a reflection of your *true* priorities. And after your routines rewrite your priorities, your priorities will then change your character. This works either way. If you read your Bible every morning, then God's Word will become your priority and will transform your life. But if you spend that time scrolling through social media instead, then entertainment, comparisons, or debate may become your priority, probably turning you into a more jealous or contentious person

> *Routines rewrite priorities, then priorities change character.*

To discard worthless routines and replace them with worthwhile ones, you must first evaluate your priorities. Not what you say they are but what they truly are. I've found three simple questions that help me do that.

1. Where do I spend my money?

As Jesus said, "Where your treasure is, there your heart will be also" (Matthew 6:21). How you actually spend your money reveals what is truly important to you. This applies to your personal finances as well as your organization's budget. You can't say that your church values leadership development if you don't spend money on training your team. Does your spending align with your stated priorities?

2. How do I spend my time?

Time is your most precious resource, and the way you spend it loudly proclaims your priorities. I'm not just talking about your scheduled time but also your discretionary time. Take some time to record a typical week and examine how closely your "time investment" reflects your priorities. Again, this applies both to your personal life and your organization's calendar.

3. Who is speaking into my life?

Who have you chosen to be your closest advisors and friends? Who are you allowing to influence you? This very much includes the books you read, shows you watch, and podcasts you listen to. Are their values aligned with your priorities?

All three of these tests represent key resources in our life—money, time, and influence—and a priority isn't a priority until it's resourced. Only when we invest in the things that matter most to us are we truly living in sync with our priorities. That is a key principle that I teach ministry leaders all the time.

> *A priority isn't a priority until it's resourced.*

Compounding Behaviors

The power of compounding interest is well known in the financial world. The idea is simple—you earn interest not just on your initial investment but also on your previous earnings. So, if a man were to hide a hundred dollars a month under his mattress for fifty years, he'd end up with $60,000. But if he invested that same amount at 5 percent compounded daily, he'd have $270,000.

The same is true of compounding behaviors. A little bit over a long time, building on itself, yields big results. Read your Bible for just ten minutes a day—even the book of Numbers and all the chronologies—and in a year you'll have read it from cover to cover. Do that every year for fifty years and you'll know the Bible better than most pastors. Give someone just ten minutes a day of your full attention and you'll have spent more than sixty hours of time together at the end of the year. On the other hand, give Instagram two hours a day, and at the end of the year you've given it a full month.

As ministry leaders, we're often discouraged because we overestimate what we can do in one day but underestimate what we can do in one year. Routines, compounded day by day, have a ridiculous impact on our influence. This is a foundational principle of the 5-Day Leader process: We're not looking for a magical overnight change but daily changes in behavior that accelerate our growth and impact over time. This is what high-impact leaders do, and there's no reason you can't do it too. I'll walk you through creating and committing to your own ridiculous routines later in the book.

CHAPTER

RESILIENT
RELATIONSHIPS

When I was a junior in high school, the guidance counselor tried to start a Big Brother, Big Sister program, but at the initial meeting no students signed up to be "Bigs." Mrs. Seibert, the counselor, was also my mom's best friend, and she used that leverage to enlist my help.

"Congratulations," Mrs. Seibert said. "You're now the president of our Big Brother, Big Sister program! And as the new president, it's your job to convince all the athletes and all the kids at the cool table to spend an hour a week playing with kids at local elementary schools."

Because I had a lot of respect for Mrs. Seibert—and have always been up for a challenge—I accepted the position. I quickly recruited enough Bigs, and then set up a meeting with an elementary principal to find our Littles. As I walked up to the school, I noticed a scrawny little fourth grader playing basketball on the playground. I watched for a moment as he shoved a bigger kid out of the way and took a shot, swearing at the bigger kid for getting in his way. This kid had a huge chip on his shoulder!

My meeting with the principal went well, and as we finished up, he asked, "Are *you* going to have a Little Brother?"

"Yeah, of course," I said.

"What age were you thinking?"

I looked out the window and saw the little Bad News Bear about to start a fight. "How about him?"

"Dale? He's all yours," the principal said with a smile and a wink.

I didn't just play basketball with Dale once a week. I learned that he came from a home full of massive dysfunction. He became not just my Little, but my little brother. We welcomed him into our house for dinners. I took him to my practices and games. If I went on a date, he went with me! When I was away at college, I even brought him on campus for a taste of college life. Throughout the years this relationship gave me two precious gifts: Dale's resilience inspired me, and our relationship forced me to develop a sense of responsibility that makes me the coach I am today. Dale went on to attend college and play basketball for his school. He became a college basketball coach too! Forty years later, we're still good friends.

I believe in relationships. Relationships are what we were created for. Relationships are where we live out Jesus's command to "love each other as I have loved you" (John 15:12). When I first started working with Josh, one of my editors, I told him, "If we finish this project with a mediocre book but a good friendship, it's a win." I firmly believe that success without relationships is a leadership failure. Reaching the pinnacle of my career with nobody by my side and realizing those most important to me have suffered collateral damage due to my ambition and drive would be the ultimate disappointment. Regardless of my income, title, or accomplishments, my biggest desire is to wake up each day knowing who is with me. Likewise, I want my family, team, and closest friends to know that I am always going to be with, and for, them.

> *Success without relationships is a leadership failure.*

Most leaders I know have some form of a purpose statement, a personal mission that defines their "why." I encourage every leader I serve to write one, but I also challenge them to develop a process statement. This defines their "how"—how they want their life and leadership to look as they fulfill their purpose. My process statement is, "I want to do hard things, with people I really care about, and I want to have fun doing it."

Keys to Resilience

When people describe their relationships, I hear adjectives like *deep, meaningful,* and *authentic.* Those are great words, but my favorite relational adjective is *resilient.* Not because I'm a former preacher and it's alliterative, but because I want relationships that will last like my forty-year friendship with Dale. I want relationships that aren't detoured by circumstance or by having a really bad day and being rude. I want relationships that endure and even embrace conflict. These resilient relationships are the ones that result in and are evidence of excellent leadership.

As a basketball coach, I scheduled thirty-two intentional conflicts a year. Thirty-two times that my players stepped on the court against a team whose agenda was literally the exact opposite of ours. Regardless of how many hours we practiced, my team could not reach their full potential without that conflict. It is during conflict and competition that we grow. Without relationships strong enough to not crumble under disagreements, confrontations, and unpleasant truths, I will never become the man, leader, father, and husband God wants me to be.

Resiliency requires four key characteristics: dignity, clarity, trust, and consistency.

1. Dignity. When we both care for the other person and welcome their skills, opinions, and contributions, we affirm their dignity. Both parties must value the other as equals before God and equally deserving of having their needs met. Dysfunctional relationships occur when one person only gives or only takes. Resilient relationships are marked by mutual give and take.

2. Clarity. Lacking clarity about expectations is one of the primary reasons for relational strife. If I have expectations for you but don't communicate them with clarity, you will be unable to meet (or challenge) them. This leads to frustration on my part and confusion on yours. We frequently avoid clarity because we're avoiding conflict, but, as my editor likes to say, "When it comes to conflict, you can either pay now or pay later with interest."

3. Trust. If we don't trust and fundamentally believe that the other person has our best interest at heart, then we will always be on guard and searching for a hidden agenda. That is not a genuine friendship. As it says in scripture, "Do nothing out of selfish ambition or vain conceit. Rather, in humility value others above yourselves" (Philippians 2:3). This is the biblical pattern of trustworthy relationships: we have to trust others and be trustworthy ourselves.

4. Consistency. Finally, a resilient relationship requires consistency over time and through trials. A one-month relationship simply does not have the depth or the fortitude of a forty-year relationship. Resiliency is both formed and demonstrated by the storms you've weathered together.

—

In my research, I've discovered two types of resilient relationships that define flourishing ministry leaders:

THE FIVE-DAY LEADER

- Relationships with those you lead
- Relationships with those who influence you

Both types of relationships have unique qualities and are vital to healthy leadership. At the same time, I'm not big into positional leadership and don't like delineating too strictly between the two. According to our organizational chart at Integrus, our executive director, Meredith King is my direct report, and it's my job to lead her. But she also is an extremely capable person and often influences me. That to say, you need both types of relationships, but you'll sometimes have them with the same person.

1. Relationships with Those You Lead

Your job as a leader is to influence others and drive outcomes. You are taking them somewhere they cannot get on their own—that's why people need leaders. Sometimes leadership is challenging people beyond their comfort zone. What's our natural reaction to resistance? We stand our ground and push back. The same is true when we stretch people in our leadership role. Even when we're pushing them for their own good to something they really want, their natural response is to dig in and push back.

> *Leadership is challenging people beyond their comfort zone.*

What I'm saying is that leadership is inherently confrontational and can naturally drive people apart. As a college coach, I met a lot of famous coaches and noticed that some of the most successful ones didn't get along with their team and their players didn't get along with each other. These coaches wouldn't even stay at the same hotel as their players.

When I was still a young coach, I was at a coaching conference in Atlanta and had the chance to meet one of these nationally known coaches.

"Hey, Coach," I said. "Congratulations on a great year!"

"*Ugh!* March was miserable!" he said. "I couldn't stand them, and they couldn't stand me, but we just kept winning. Every time we won, I'd think, *S***! Three more days with these guys.*"

I came back from that encounter and said to Ronda, "I will never bring a kid into our locker room that we wouldn't bring into our living room." And I didn't. Success at the expense of healthy relationships is not worth the cost to me. Not only does an antagonistic relationship like those coaches and players had harm them personally, but it also prevents true leadership and growth.

Life is all about the journey together. In his classic leadership book, *Good to Great*, Jim Collins talks about getting the right people on the bus and into the right seats.[1] I would add—if the people on the bus don't like each other, it's going to be a very long trip.

Make no mistake, I didn't go easy on my players. I pushed them all the harder because I cared about them and was trying to lead them where they wanted to go. The reason they responded well to my pushing was that I *intentionally* built resilient relationships with them. I committed to spending two minutes with them outside of practice for every one minute we spent in practice—meeting them for coffee, dropping chocolate chip cookies off at their dorm rooms, eating in the cafeteria with them, going on road trips, going to the movies, whatever. Again, leadership is inherently confrontational and will naturally drive your team away from you. The harder you push your team, the harder you must work to pull them close.

> *The harder you push your team, the harder*
> *you must work to pull them close.*

When it comes to resilient relationships, Jesus is our greatest example of leadership. He certainly pushed the disciples further than they could go on their own, challenging their ideas about God and teaching them brand-new ways to live. And how often do we see him getting frustrated by their lack of faith or childish squabbles about who was greatest? But at the same time, he spent three years developing resilient relationships with them, working, eating, and sleeping alongside them and treating them as friends.

2. Relationships with Those Who Influence You

I've known leaders who do well at building resilient relationships with those they lead, but struggle making friends outside their organization. For them it feels emotionally safer to avoid peer-to-peer relationships. But relational dynamics are different when you're signing someone's paycheck! You need to have relationships with people who can speak freely in your life.

As an only child in a single-parent home, I was alone a lot and learned the art and the benefit of observing others.

I remember thinking while in middle school, *What kind of high schooler do I want to be?* And then I looked for a good example to follow. Then, when I was in college, I paid attention to young men with their families. Later, as a young man myself, I was fortunate that some incredible men invested in me as friends and mentors. In each stage of life, observing others taught me about the actions, habits, and routines that would and would not result in the kind of life I wanted to live. I am a far better person because I intentionally looked—and continue to look—for people who can influence me.

In addition, I've intentionally sought diverse influences throughout my life. God loves variety—just look at all the different types of flowers in the fields or people walking through an airport—and having a variety of relationships is one of the most valuable things we can possess as a leader. Without that, we are at risk of creating an echo chamber for ourselves, where we are never challenged and, therefore, never grow.

Last year, I made a year-long commitment not to read a single book written by middle-aged white men, because I'm a middle-aged white male. I read books by people twenty years older than me and twenty years younger. I read books written by women and from authors of every race, religion, and political viewpoint. I didn't agree with everything I read, but it was unbelievably valuable to me to see the world from different perspectives. It's good to have my beliefs and convictions challenged on a regular basis, because it stretches my understanding of the world and clarifies my beliefs and priorities. Reading books by and about people different from me for an entire year was eye opening and life changing—and this is the same thing I look for in resilient relationships. Seeking relationships with people who have different perspectives can challenge, influence, and lead us somewhere we cannot go on our own.

—

Resilient relationships are costly. They cost us time, they cost us emotional bandwidth, and they cost us the safety of emotional isolation. Superficial relationships are cheap, costing only a friendly wave at church or a "like" on Facebook. We aren't at risk of getting hurt, and if they offend us, we can just unfriend them. It's like the difference between a pop-up tent and a custom-built home. The tent is quick, provides some comfort, and is easily replaced with the newest model. A custom-built home takes time, effort, and a considerable investment. Resilient relationships are worth the investment.

SECOND HALF

GAME TIME

CHAPTER

THE FIVE-DAY
LEADER PROCESS

Early smartphones, like the Blackberry, were a great idea—a portable device that combined your phone, contacts, email, and calendar. But they were not well executed. They were heavy, they didn't have a touch screen, and they didn't easily support the use of apps. Then, in 2007, Steve Jobs introduced the iPhone—a great idea, well executed. All these years later, it's hard to remember how revolutionary it was. A smartphone that was both powerful and easy to use truly changed the world.

One of the greatest compliments our Integrus team has ever received was when a group of leaders called our processes "insanely practical and incredibly effective." I want to make leadership "insanely practical and incredibly effective."

A couple years ago I felt led to start the year by setting aside time specifically to draw closer to God and examine my life and ministry. During those life-changing days, two significant experiences refined my understanding of leaders and leadership. The first was a conversation that I had with a person on a flight to New York. As we were talking, I explained to him what I did. He seemed very interested and asked this intriguing question: "Who are the five most impressive leaders that you have ever worked with?" After a bit of reflection, I shared a few names and went on to explain why each one was unique and exceptional.

After settling into my hotel that night, I began thinking through my answer to his question and started two lists on a legal pad. On one side I listed all the exceptional leaders I had encountered, and on the other side I wrote down why I considered them unique, what behaviors caused them to be successful in a meaningful way. Creating that list opened my eyes to the tremendous value of relentless growth, ridiculous routines, and resilient relationships. Yes, that was the beginning of the 3Rs of leadership that I've just shared with you.

This season of intense reflection was also the first time I heard the quote I shared with you back in chapter 3: "A great concept can be explained in five minutes but discussed for five days."

As I pondered that idea, I thought about the many things I'd learned from the remarkable ministry, business, sports, and nonprofit leaders I admired. I asked God to show me a way to communicate what I had learned about excellent leadership in a way that could be explained succinctly and executed simply. I asked God for a way to teach leadership that would be insanely practical and incredibly effective.

A week later I went to my daughter's apartment, sat at her kitchen table, and wrote for two days straight. As I prayed about these things, the Lord shaped the 5-Day Leader process in my heart, the coalescence of more than thirty years of studying, practicing, and teaching leadership.

My heart was to create a simple process that anyone can implement. I also wanted to make it repetitive so they could repeat the process and continue to grow over seasons of weeks, months, and years. Whether you are a ministry leader looking to grow personally or looking for content for your weekly staff meetings, the 5-Day Leader process can be applied to any ministry setting. And you don't need to have a typical Monday-through-Friday workweek. I know most ministry leaders might shift this schedule to fit the rhythms of your team. In any case, you'll find these workday themes are actionable.

The Five-Day Leader Process

- Move the Needle Monday
- Tough Tuesday
- WOW Wednesday
- Throwback Thursday
- Finish Strong Friday

These themes create a framework for how to approach each weekday. For instance, did you know that Mondays can be our most productive day of the week? Instead of treating it like a blah day, we're going to use it to charge into the new week. For each day of the week, I will give you three action items so you can focus on relentless growth, ridiculous routines, and resilient relationships.

This isn't like a five-day cleanse, where you go through it once and then set it aside until you need another boost. I want this to become a lifestyle, just as it has been for me. These five daily themes define how I approach every weekday. Together, this approach can create new habits, compounding behaviors that continue to build your credibility and influence.

Also, unlike a five-day cleanse, these new habits won't leave you miserable and longing to go back to "normal." Instead, they can reshape your normal into something you enjoy and embrace fresh each week. None of these challenges are overly difficult or complex, but when done consistently at a high level, they will create the resources you need to shepherd those you lead.

Here's how I want you to proceed. Choose the Monday you want to take action and implement the challenges we give you for that day of the week. I've included three tracks for you to choose from.

Track 1: Take one action every day of the week.
Track 2: Take two actions every day of the week.
Track 3: Take three actions every weekday.

Each of us is different and will approach these exercises differently. And what if you don't work a standard Monday through Friday workweek? Many pastors, for instance, take Mondays or Fridays and (hopefully) Saturdays off. As you dig into each weekday's theme, figure out how to best apply its spirit to your work schedule.

My teammate Meredith would add one final thing: We are all under an umbrella of mercy. Some weeks may be easy and others hard. The week I worked on this chapter was one of those insane weeks where I was happy just to make it to bed before sunrise and had to let several action items go. Success isn't defined by individual days but a lifetime's trajectory. If you consistently grow in each of these habits over time, then it's a win.

Success isn't defined by individual days but a lifetime's trajectory.

Are you ready? It's game time!

The Five-Day Leader Process

	Track 1	Track 2	Track 3
Move the Needle Monday	☐ Engage one Truth Teller and ask for their feedback.	☐ Engage one Truth Teller and ask for their feedback. ☐ Define your three highest-value activities for the week and write them down in order of priority.	☐ Engage one Truth Teller and ask for their feedback. ☐ Define your three highest-value activities for the week and write them down in order of priority. ☐ Celebrate two people in your life or in the life of someone you care about.
Tough Tuesday	☐ Add one hour to your day and devote it to your growth.	☐ Add one hour to your day and devote it to your growth. ☐ The Plus-One Challenge: push yourself to "add one" to whatever you do today.	☐ Add one hour to your day and devote it to your growth. ☐ The Plus-One Challenge: push yourself to "add one" to whatever you do today. ☐ Say "no" or "not yet" to at least one task, request, opportunity, or invitation, and invest the time saved into the relationships that matter most.

WOW Wednesday	❑ Find one way to make the people you serve say, "Wow!"	❑ Find one way to make the people you serve say, "Wow!" ❑ Try something new that takes you way out of your comfort zone.	❑ Find one way to make the people you serve say, "Wow!" ❑ Try something new that takes you way out of your comfort zone. ❑ Give a gift to build a relationship.
Throwback Thursday	❑ Apply the "think it twice" rule.	❑ Apply the "think it twice" rule. ❑ Write down one thing you've learned in the past week.	❑ Apply the "think it twice" rule. ❑ Write down one thing you've learned in the past week. ❑ Reach out to someone you haven't talked to in the last ninety days.
Finish Strong Friday	❑ Complete one task as though it were in front of a cheering crowd.	❑ Complete one task as though it were in front of a cheering crowd. ❑ Finish as many things as possible.	❑ Complete one task as though it were in front of a cheering crowd. ❑ Finish as many things as possible. ❑ Give a specific affirmation to two people.

CHAPTER

MOVE THE NEEDLE
MONDAY

Why are New Year's resolutions so popular? While we know intellectually that January 1 is an arbitrary date, people who make New Year's resolutions believe a change in the calendar may prompt a change in behavior. The past can be set aside, and we can try again. But we don't have to wait 365 days before renewing our commitment to growth.

I believe every Monday is a mini-New Year's Day. Even if the previous week was a train wreck, you can receive God's grace for the new week and embrace a fresh start. As the apostle Paul said, "One thing I do: Forgetting what is behind and straining toward what is ahead, I press on toward the goal to win the prize for which God has called me heavenward in Christ Jesus" (Philippians 3:13–14).

Forget everything you've heard about Mondays. Studies have shown that Mondays and Tuesdays are typically our most productive days of the week.[1] Rather than squandering all that productivity on tasks with negligible long-term impact, funnel it toward moving the needle. What does that mean? "Moving the needle" simply means to get better, to make some progress. I want to go to bed every Monday night having improved from last week. If I don't, that's okay because I'm under an umbrella of mercy. But my goal is to make Monday my forward-momentum day.

This isn't just about capitalizing on Monday's productivity, though. Monday sets the direction and tone for the week. If you nail it on Monday, you're far more likely to keep nailing it the rest of the week. I intentionally avoid making any low-productivity appointments (including personal things like dentist appointments) on Monday as to not disrupt my flow. I also plan my Monday the night before so I can hit the ground running. Monday is your best day, so don't waste it.

> **MOVE THE NEEDLE MONDAY MINDSET**
> Move the Needle Monday is my day to accept a full measure of God's grace for the week ahead. I will learn from the past week, but I won't be held back by my failures nor rest on my success. I will press forward and make progress. I will move the needle.

Now let's apply *move the needle* with three action items.

1. Engage one "Truth Teller" and ask for their feedback.

As I said in chapter 5, the first step of growth is confrontation. I'm challenging you to seek out that confrontation. Is this painful? Potentially, but it's less painful than being blindsided by it—as when my friend told me I was being too hard on my children.

Truth Tellers are those you have a resilient relationship with, who know you well enough to see your flaws and love you enough to have your best interests at heart. As scripture says,

"Wounds from a friend can be trusted, but an enemy multiplies kisses" (Proverbs 27:6).

Who has permission to speak into your life? Who are the people who see past your Instagram pictures to the real person underneath and give godly council?

If you can't immediately come up with at least three people, some of whom you are not related to, then I'm going to be a Truth Teller to you: That must change. The most destructive leaders I've ever seen are the ones who only surrounded themselves with people either too afraid or too awestruck to speak hard truths.

Assuming you have Truth Tellers in your life, how do you intentionally engage them? It isn't enough to say, "Hey, Truth Teller! Can you give me some feedback?" That will seldom give you the sort of information needed to move your needle forward. Begin by asking God to lead you to the right Truth Teller, to guide their words, and to prepare you for what they see.

When you approach them, explain your desire to move the needle and grow, then ask a specific question.

Personal Questions

Here are some questions I routinely ask my Truth Tellers:

- What is one thing I can be doing to be a better husband, father, or friend?
- When do you feel loved well by me?
- If you could change one thing about me or our relationship, what would that be?
- Am I giving you all the love and leadership that you want from me?
- Are you seeing anything in me that could compromise my walk with Jesus or my witness for him?

Professional Questions

Ask them just one question like these, then get quiet and listen:

- What is one thing I am doing to make your job harder?
- What is one thing I could do to make your job easier?
- What do I do that frustrates you?
- In the past three months, when have you felt well led?
- How can I better support you and your success?

What you do after they answer is the single most important part of this challenge. Meredith tells how she used to work for a leader (not me, I promise) who talked a big game about wanting feedback. But when he asked for input on a specific project and she gave it, he embarrassed her in front of the entire team. The leader said one thing, but his actions communicated another—and she never offered him honest feedback again.

Your immediate response to your Truth Teller's feedback will set the course for all future interactions. No matter what they say, no matter whether you agree with them or not, respond with a gracious "thank you" and perhaps a clarifying question. Then remind yourself that your identity is rooted in your position as a child of God, not in what you do. Carefully evaluate their feedback. Even if the particulars are mistaken, you almost certainly can find a kernel you needed to hear. Reread the "Four Steps of Growth" in chapter 5, then commit yourself to a course of action to move your needle in that area.

2. Define your three highest-value activities for the week, and write them down in order of priority.

I am not a fan of to-do lists. They tend to be listed in the order I identified the needs, not their relative importance. So "give Lonestar a bath" (my Yorkshire terrier—can you tell I live in

Texas?) could end up being done before "identify the biggest holes in our outreach strategy." Human nature is to use easy tasks to avoid the difficult ones. That is why I said Monday's productivity shouldn't be wasted on dentist appointments—or washing the dog.

Early Monday morning (before you get to your office) or Sunday evening, ask yourself this: what is the single thing this week that will have the greatest impact on those I lead and my area of responsibility? Write that down, then add the second- and third-highest-value activities. Then make a specific plan for tackling them. Keep this list in front of you all week long and don't allow yourself to be distracted by lower-value activities. Remember, it's not a priority until it's resourced with an investment of your time or energy. As you cross things off your list, continue adding new high-value activities.

What about all those low-value tasks that still must get done? First, make sure you really should be the one to do the task. (I'll give you a tool for that in Tuesday's Resilient Relationship challenge.) Then create a separate list of the ones that are truly your responsibility, and hammer away on them in spare low-productivity moments.

One trick I like to use to accomplish some of my low-value tasks is called "habit stacking." I became aware of this concept when I read James Clear's book *Atomic Habits*, and it is a brilliant way to increase efficiency and effectiveness. Habit stacking occurs when we stack one habit or task on top of another.[2] For example, I have extended family members I like to have conversations with on a regular basis, but I rarely have time to connect during the workweek. On Saturday I will habit stack by putting in my earbuds and calling my mother-in-law while giving my dog, Lonestar, his bath. Or, if I have nonurgent correspondence that needs to be addressed in my inbox, I will save all those emails for a time when I want to sit down and watch a game. Instead of occupying my hands by eating chips and queso while I watch the game, I stack the two activities.

3. Celebrate two people in your life or in the life of someone you care about.

This one is not difficult, and it's also fun and life-giving to you and the recipient. I've always been bothered that so many people wait until someone's "celebration of life" to celebrate their life. The goal today is to celebrate another person with a simple word of encouragement or acknowledgment that you give in person or via text, phone call, handwritten note, or email.

The specific term for this action is called *affirmation*. I love that the root word in *affirmation* is *firm*, which means "to make solid." When we celebrate a positive behavior in someone's life with an affirmation, it means we are potentially making the behavior more solid, or more permanent, in them. It means we are making our appreciation and affection for that person more definitive.

You could celebrate a coworker who did a great job on a project, a teacher who goes above and beyond, your pastor, your spouse, or one of your children. As leaders, we must be intentional about celebrating others or else this practice will get lost in the busyness of day-to-day life.

This challenge is genuinely my favorite part of Move the Needle Monday. By Saturday, I'm already thinking about who I can celebrate on Monday, and I can rarely stop at two!

Moment of Grace

As I've already said, this is not a self-help book. I repeat it because whenever we strive to grow, we will encounter constant temptation to rely on ourselves. So, I'm going to include a little "moment of grace" with each day, a reminder that this is all about what God does in and with us, not what we do for God.

If you have ever questioned the value of affirmation, let me direct you to Matthew 3:16–17. The Bible tells us that as Jesus was being baptized and coming up out of the water, a voice from heaven said, "This is my Son, whom I love; with him I am well pleased." Ponder that for a moment. In this passage we see God the Father *affirming* Jesus the Son, one member of the Trinity to another. If God places this much value on affirmation of someone who needed none, how much more should we affirm the people we serve?

Game Time!

Are you ready for your new favorite—and most productive—day of the week? All the planning and theory don't matter if you don't put it into practice, so I'll conclude each day with some reflection questions. You can use this personally or bring it to your team and work through them together.

Discussion Questions

1. Going in, what was your disposition toward Mondays: miserable, mediocre, or motivated? Did this chapter change that? How?

2. I said every Monday is a mini-New Year's Day. What is the value of symbolic fresh starts? How have you been able to use fresh starts to your benefit in the past?

3. What does *move the needle* mean to you? How would your leadership be different if you got a little bit better each week?

4. Why is it important to start your week out strong? Think of a recent strong Monday, as well as a weak one. How did they affect the rest of your week?

5. (Return to this question after completing a Move the Needle Monday.) How did embracing these challenges affect your feelings about Mondays? Are you now feeling more motivated for Mondays?

MOVE THE NEEDLE MONDAY

When will you attempt your first Move the Needle Monday?

Track 1

- ☐ Engage one Truth Teller and ask for their feedback.

Track 2

- ☐ Engage one Truth Teller and ask for their feedback.
- ☐ Define your three highest-value activities for the week and write them down in order of priority.

Track 3

- ☐ Engage one Truth Teller and ask for their feedback.
- ☐ Define your three highest-value activities for the week and write them down in order of priority.
- ☐ Celebrate two people in your life or in the life of someone you care about.

10

TOUGH TUESDAY

———

Most of us love a good challenge. Childhood is filled with challenges like, "I bet you can't throw that over your house," or "I'm going to read more books than you this year!" or "Let's race to the stop sign." Part of our growth process then was challenging ourselves, stretching ourselves, and even discovering our limits.

As we get older, our desire for comfort begins competing with our love of challenge. We still enjoy the thrill of setting a personal best, but we may enjoy hitting the snooze button even more. But comfort is not our life's purpose.

I've had the privilege of having conversations with several Navy SEALs, and they taught me the meaning of their motto, "The only easy day was yesterday." They didn't join the SEALs to be comfortable. They wanted the challenge. They wanted to do hard things. They wanted to make a difference in the world. To make all that happen, they crave the challenge of a day that's even harder than yesterday.

Welcome to Tough Tuesday, designed to be one of the harder days of the 5-Day Leader process—a tough but rewarding day. As I mentioned in the last chapter, Mondays and Tuesdays are typically our most productive days of the week. Monday's challenge was to start the week strong. Now, instead of easing up, it's time to work all the harder to create an upward trajectory for the rest of the week. Get uncomfortable. Defy your limits. Just for one day a week, pretend you are a SEAL. Keep reading to figure out exactly how.

TOUGH TUESDAY MINDSET

Tough Tuesday is my day to build off yesterday's momentum and push myself to go even further. For one day, I will seek challenge and not comfort. I will do hard things. I will be tough.

---

1. Add one hour to your day and devote it to your growth.

One of ministry leaders' most common frustrations is their inability to make time to read for professional growth. In fact, some of them have told me that they have gone years without reading a book on leadership or their particular industry. Leadership expert Mike Myatt proposes that the one common denominator all great leaders share is their intentionality to read voraciously. Here's what Mike has to say about leaders who read: "The greatest leaders throughout history have been nothing short of relentless in their pursuit of knowledge. If you are anything less then you are not only cheating yourself, but you're also cheating your organization."[1]

I find that high-impact leaders aren't any less busy than you, but they still find time to learn and grow. That's why I am challenging you to add an hour to your Tough Tuesday so you can make the time to grow.

Where will you find that extra hour? Get up one hour earlier, stay up later, spend one less hour in front of your TV, or skip your lunch break. This is only once a week. You can find one hour in plenty of places if you look hard enough. I'm a morning guy, so I just get up an hour earlier. The house is quiet, and I can focus. Dedicating your lunch break to growth is a popular option too.

Just as setting out your exercise clothes the night before greatly increases the likelihood of completing your morning workout, creating a "Tuesday Growth" folder (real or virtual) will help you make the best use of your hour. Whenever you come across a valuable book, podcast, article, or TED Talk, put it into that folder. You might find yourself diving into it on other days too. That's a win!

2. The Plus-One Challenge: push yourself to "add one" to whatever you do today.

Normally run thirty minutes on the treadmill? Run thirty-one. Getting a dozen roses for your wife? Get thirteen (you're not superstitious, are you?). Buying a coffee at Starbucks? Buy another one for the person behind you. Planning to call three donors? Call four. Push yourself to exceed your own expectations. There is almost always a gap between what we think we can do and what we're truly capable of. On Tough Tuesdays, we come closer to discovering our actual limits. Consistently embrace this challenge, and you'll watch your baseline steadily increase.

The ministry leaders I'm investing in through coaching consistently say that the Plus-One Challenge is one of their favorites and the most fulfilling. Why? Because no one wants to be average. And certainly, no ministry leader wants to be average. We love the challenge of setting new personal bests and raising the bar on our performance. And because leadership is influence, our growth will inspire and empower those we lead. I often tell groups I speak to that you can't inspire others if you're living an uninspired life. The activities we engage in on Tough Tuesday will serve to inspire us and others.

3. Say "no" or "not yet" to at least one task, request, opportunity, or invitation, and invest the time saved into the relationships that matter most.

In chapter 1, I said this book is for leaders who feel underresourced. What is the number one resource most leaders lack? Time. And what it the first thing we usually shortchange when we run out of time? Relationships. In the past week how many times have you wanted to connect with someone but couldn't find the time? I'm talking about something far more critical than catching up with an old friend over coffee. In my experience, leaders cannot activate their skills or knowledge unless they have invested into key relationships. This is true in our family life as well. In short, leadership failure is usually a relationship failure.

> *Leadership failure is usually a relationship failure.*

Time management is a myth. It's 9:20 a.m. as I write this. In ten minutes it will be 9:30, and nothing I can do will manage that. But I *can* manage my choices. Every time we say yes to something new, we push something else out. I've learned to evaluate every request and opportunity and assign it to one of three categories, using traffic lights as my visuals:

Green Lights. These are the things only I can do. This list is much shorter than I used to believe, but the things on it deserve my highest attention. I cannot delegate away being a husband to Ronda or father to my children. I cannot delegate away the responsibility for my health, friendships, or spiritual growth. And (despite what too many leaders think) I cannot delegate away my relationships with the people I lead. In short, you cannot delegate away relationships.

> *You cannot delegate away relationships.*

Yellow Lights. These are the things I feel I should do, but they could be done by someone else or be left undone. Going to an acquaintance's birthday party, leading a Bible study, attending a conference. Yellow lights are tough to resist because they are good things, and you feel guilty for saying no. They frequently make you feel good about yourself (such as being asked to serve on the board of a well-respected nonprofit) but aren't in line with your priorities. Yellow lights are not an automatic no, but they must be carefully evaluated, or they could displace a green light.

Red Lights. Like the thirty hours a week that the CEO from chapter 6 spent playing video games, these are the obvious nos. If you're serious about growing as a leader, you've already started dealing with time wasters.

I'm not saying leaders aren't allowed to play. Relaxation is vital to our well-being. The key is scaling them to appropriate levels. For example, I love golf, but now I often play nine holes instead of eighteen. I still get out and have fun—if anything, a half round leaves me more refreshed than a full round—but I've added two hours to my day.

As a pastor I have had the privilege and responsibility of ministering to many people at the end of their lives. As people realize their time on earth is limited, they often share their regrets. Their greatest regret is almost always not giving more time to their significant relationships.

If you are a capable person, you will never lack worthwhile things to do. High-impact leaders focus only on the people and projects that are most important for *them* to embrace. Accept this challenge, and say no to at least one yellow-light or red-light activity so you can spend more time loving, inspiring, and influencing the people you care about most.

Moment of Grace

The better we understand God's grace in our lives, the easier it is to say no to some of the requests that come our way. Remember how the apostle Paul described his ministry:

> What, after all, is Apollos? And what is Paul? Only servants, through whom you came to believe—as the Lord has assigned to each his task. I planted the seed, Apollos watered it, but God has been making it grow. So neither the one who plants nor the one who waters is anything, but only God, who makes things grow. (1 Corinthians 3:5–7)

Paul focused on his specific calling, knowing that Apollos was focusing on his. And above that, God was the one accomplishing it all. So even as you push yourself to do hard things on Tough Tuesday, never forget that God is still on his throne. Receive his grace to do more than you did yesterday and receive his grace when you fall short.

Are you ready for this challenge? Are you ready to redefine some limits? If so, then as the apostle Paul says, let's "run the race marked out for us" (Hebrews 12:1) by getting intentional about Tough Tuesday.

Discussion Questions

1. What has been your typical attitude toward challenges that push you beyond your perceived limits? Has it been "Bring it on!" or have you often been reluctant to push your boundaries?

2. What value is found in challenging yourself in specific areas? Reflect on a time that you did embrace a challenge. Did growth occur? Why or why not?

3. Why is it important for leaders to be willing to do tough things?

4. Has saying no to people and opportunities been a challenge for you in the past? Can you think of a time when you should have said no to an opportunity or obligation but didn't? What was the cost? On the flip side, can you remember a time when you did say no and saw benefits to setting a healthy boundary?

TOUGH TUESDAY

When will you attempt your first Tough Tuesday?

Track 1

☐ Add one hour to your day and devote it to your growth.

Track 2

☐ Add one hour to your day and devote it to your growth.
☐ The Plus-One Challenge: push yourself to add one to whatever you do today.

Track 3

☐ Add one hour to your day and devote it to your growth.
☐ The Plus-One Challenge: push yourself to add one to whatever you do today.
☐ Say no or not yet to at least one task, request, opportunity, or invitation, and invest the time saved into the relationships that matter most.

CHAPTER 11

WOW WEDNESDAY

Pet peeve warning: I hate calling Wednesday "Hump Day," as if work is a chore and I can't wait for the weekend. Scripture reminds us to "serve the LORD with gladness!" (Psalm 100:2 NKJV). Moreover, we're told to "work willingly at whatever you do, as though you were working for the LORD rather than for people" (Colossians 3:23 NLT). I'm grateful for the weekends but look forward to each new week that I have the privilege of doing the work God has given me. I *get* to coach ministry leaders who go on to impact thousands of people. And you—you are loving and leading others, influencing lives, and impacting communities for Christ. You *get* to make a difference in people's lives.

Have you ever heard the joke, "Leadership would be great ... if it weren't for the people"? Worse, have you said it? The longer you serve people, the easier it is to get jaded and the easier it is to get into a rut. WOW Wednesday is about getting out of that rut and remembering that it is an honor to serve God's people. Every Wednesday we have two days in the rearview mirror and two more ahead of us, so let's make it sparkle just a little more. Take things to a new level. Surprise the people you lead. Surprise yourself.

> **WOW WEDNESDAY MINDSET**
> WOW Wednesday is my day to get out of a rut and add a
> special touch to what I do. It is my day bring the *wow* back
> into what I do. My work isn't a burden to endure. It's my
> privilege and joy to serve God and his children.

1. Find one way to make the people you serve say, "Wow!"

If you had to wait in line for an hour, would you prefer to do
so at Disneyland or your local DMV? The reason for the better
experience at Disneyland is that the DMV knows you have to deal
with them regardless of how poorly lit the office is or grumpy
the clerks are. On the other hand, Disney recognizes that you're
spending a lot of money to be there. One thinks they're doing *you*
a favor, while the other knows you're doing *them* a favor.

Think about your church, ministry, or nonprofit. Do you
think your ministry feels more like the DMV or Disneyland to
the people you serve? In his book *Inside the Magic Kingdom: Seven
Keys to Disney's Success*, Tom Connellan examines Disneyland's
fanatical attention to their guests' experience and what other
businesses can learn from it. It all comes down the Golden Rule—
treat people like you'd want to be treated. If Disney can do that
(and have a 70 percent return rate[1]) for the sake of making money,
how much more can we do it for the sake of glorifying God and
honoring the flock he entrusted to us?

I've learned that asking the right questions is usually a great
stimulus for growth, so I want you to take one area of your
organization and ask, "How can we make this better, faster,
easier, cheaper, or more enjoyable?" Use Wednesdays to remind
yourself that it's a privilege to serve, then focus on finding a way
to exceed expectations. It can be something simple, like allowing

the mom with a pair of restless kids to go ahead of you in line or ordering a dessert to go and giving it to the desk clerk when you return to the hotel. In some cases, it can be something much bigger. One year, when Christmas Day fell on a Wednesday, our church determined that they would hold a "reverse Christmas" event and asked everyone in the congregation to simply ask one person who would normally give them a gift to give a donation of equal amount to Charity Water instead of purchasing a gift. With that one WOW Wednesday, we were able to provide clean water to an entire African village—hundreds of people—for at least the next twenty years!

Something crucial to remember as you think about creating a "wow experience" is that it doesn't just apply to your work. As you read the last few paragraphs, your mind probably went to your office or a place where you volunteer. But remember, the most important place we can create wow experiences is in our own home, with the people we love the most. You know that special treat your spouse loves for dessert, or how much they enjoy a good back rub or foot massage. You know your children's love language or how excited they would be to stay up just a little later to watch a game with you. You know the things that will wow your people. WOW Wednesdays are about actually doing them. One of my favorite memories of my dad is when he showed up at my first-grade classroom one afternoon to take me home and watch the World Series with him. That was certainly a wow experience!

2. Try something new that takes you way out of your comfort zone.

If you choose to get out of your comfort zone, it will mean that failure is an option. In fact, if you consistently try something new without failure, then you're probably not stretching yourself enough. The objective here is to try. One Wednesday I went to a yoga class—that stretched me in more ways than one! You don't want to get to the end of your life and regret things you wished you'd done, relationships you should've invested in, risks you wanted to take, or the opportunities that passed you by. If we don't develop the skill of stretching, we run the risk of having more regrets than memories.

Next time you have a wild thought that's followed by, *There's no way I could ever do that*, write it down in your "Stretch Assignment" file. Things like:

- Email that author who really inspired me.
- Sign up for a marathon.
- Reach out to an organization I'd love to partner with.
- Write an inspirational message and post it on social media.
- Experiment with a new software.
- Go skydiving.

Again, failure is an option (except for skydiving). This isn't about what you accomplish, but rather the habit of stretching yourself and trying something new. It's about seeking new opportunities or facing new challenges. The goal is to disrupt the comfortable in your life—rearrange a room at home, have a conversation with someone that will challenge you, try to cook a meal that feels way outside of your skill set.

Developing a mindset and habit of stretching yourself has benefits that go way beyond just you. Remember that leadership is a behavior, and it is our behavior that influences others. A significant role in leadership is inspiring those you lead, and it's hard to inspire others if you live an uninspired life.

It is hard to inspire others if you live an uninspired life.

In her book *A Return to Love,* Marianne Williamson sums up this idea so beautifully when she wrote, "And as we let our own light shine, we unconsciously give other people permission to do the same. As we are liberated from our own fear, our presence automatically liberates others."[2]

3. Give a gift to build a relationship.

This is perhaps my favorite of all the challenges in the 5-Day Leader process. Jesus knew what he was talking about when he said, "It is more blessed to give than to receive" (Acts 20:35)! I know of a pastor who traveled with his family to Mexico. They all brought spending money, but after deciding he didn't need to buy more stuff, he gave away his money in the form of generous tips. He enjoyed his money more than anyone else in his family.

After telling the parable of the dishonest steward, Jesus said:

> I tell you, use worldly wealth to gain friends for yourselves, so that when it is gone, you will be welcomed into eternal dwellings. Whoever can be trusted with very little can also be trusted with much, and whoever is dishonest with very little will also be dishonest with much. So if you have not been trustworthy in handling worldly wealth, who will trust you with true riches? And if you have not been trustworthy with someone else's property, who will give you property of your own? (Luke 16:9–12)

What does it mean to "use worldly wealth to gain friends"? Gifts open the door for relationships. That is a basic principle of life. Giving is frequently done in a manipulative way (as Proverbs 19:6 warns), but when the gift is genuinely given for the benefit of the other person, Jesus says you are making a wise investment.

Using earthly wealth to build a relationship that will last for eternity shows that you're trustworthy with true riches.

You may be thinking, *There are fifty-two weeks in a year, which means fifty-two gifts—and I'm on a budget.* I understand. I have a budget too! Not every gift has to be purchased. When I read a book that really impacts me, I always give it to a friend who I think would enjoy it as much as I did. Not every gift has to be expensive.

Here are some great examples of affordable gift-giving ideas that I have witnessed:

- A leader gives one of her employees a gift card for a small amount to a coffee shop and tells them that they can have an extra hour to come in to work one morning so the employee can sit and enjoy that coffee with a friend or a good book.
- One leader started to notice that many of his younger team members had stickers on their computers, so he started buying stickers with their favorite teams or sayings on them.
- A school principal gives out candy bars with silly notes attached, like "Our teachers are the best in the MILKY WAY."
- Some leaders make treats for their staff on a regular basis.
- Small gifts for a team members' children or their pets can have a great impact.

The bottom line when it comes to gifts is simply thought and effort. Gifts that reflect a little bit of thought and some degree of effort are almost always well received and appreciated.

It's important to model mindfulness and generosity to those we lead. Think back to a time when someone gave you a gift that affected you far beyond its value. Today, look for ways to do that for someone else. This gift doesn't have to be expensive or elaborate, just thoughtful and intentional. Prayerfully consider how to build a resilient relationship through a gift.

Moment of Grace

Speaking of prayer, if you are satisfied doing everything to your own ability, you don't need prayer. Prayer invites God to come in and do it to his ability. Again, grace means relying on God to do what only he can do. Prayer is where the real wow factor comes in. Bathe your Wednesdays in prayer, asking God to equip you to do far more than you could do on your own. Here's something you could pray:

God, thank you for the privilege of leading the people in my care. Please keep my heart soft, and show me how to best serve them. Today especially, show me how to wow them with unexpectedly excellent service, inspiration as I stretch past my personal limits, or a gift that shows just how much I value them. Make it clear to me what would benefit them most, and give me what I need to do just that. In Jesus's name, amen.

Discussion Questions

1. Describe the best experience you've ever had as a church or ministry attendee. What made the experience so special?

2. If you could change anything about the experience of the people you serve, what would you change, and why?

3. Describe the last time you tried something new. What was it? How did it go?

4. Why do you think it's hard to try new things in ministry work? What prevents you or your team from making significant improvements?

5. In this moment, does leadership and ministry feel like a "get to" or a "have to"? How about over the last month and year? What factors are driving your answer?

6. If it's been more "have to" than "get to," has that felt more like cynicism, discouragement, or exhaustion? What steps are needed to prevent burnout?

WOW WEDNESDAY

When will you attempt your first WOW Wednesday?

_____

Track 1

❏ Find one way to make the people you serve say, "Wow!"

Track 2

❏ Find one way to make the people you serve say, "Wow!"
❏ Try something new that takes you way out of your comfort zone.

Track 3

❏ Find one way to make the people you serve say, "Wow!"
❏ Try something new that takes you way out of your comfort zone.
❏ Give a gift to build a relationship.

12

THROWBACK THURSDAY

O n Monday, we tried to move the needle and set the bar for the rest of the week. On Tuesday, we dug in deep and gave an extra effort. Wednesday, we focused on doing things well. Thursday is our day to catch our breath and reflect.

In the movie *Fifty First Dates*, Adam Sandler's character is dating Lucy, played by Drew Barrymore.[1] The twist is that Lucy suffers from short-term memory loss, and every morning she completely forgets who he is. It's a funny, sweet movie, but it's also permeated by sadness, a perpetual sense of loss. Years of memories, experiences, and accumulated wisdom are lost forever. That's what we try to avoid on Thursday. Lucy's memory loss came from a car accident, but ours can come from not taking time to remember.

As a leader, you already know it's important to reflect on the past and the lessons you've learned, but life gets busy. That is the purpose of Throwback Thursday. Our goal is to take advantage of this natural lull and turn a typically unproductive day into one with long-lasting value. Today's challenges are easier than most, yet incredibly rich.

> **THROWBACK THURSDAY MINDSET**
> Throwback Thursday is my day to catch my breath and reflect on the previous week. By intentionally examining the past, I will gain wisdom and find opportunities for the future

1. Apply the "think it twice" rule.

Because I'm an act-first guy rather than a think-first, the Bible creates an interesting dilemma for me. On one hand, the value of self-control is a constant theme, specifically in Proverbs and in passages like James 1:19. On the other hand, the word *go* is used more than fourteen hundred times! There's the dilemma: when do I demonstrate self-control and when should I go?

Imagine you have someone on your team who has missed a deadline. They made a commitment to deliver on a project by a certain time, and it is now past due. What is your typical response: (1) address it immediately, (2) get frustrated but avoid the problem, or (3) make a mental note to talk to them the next time it happens—and actually do it?

Recently a friend and I were talking about this. I'm in the first group. I see a problem and it's ready, fire, aim. He's more in the second group. He's still steadying his aim long after the situation has come and gone. Very, very few people are in the third group. This is where the "think it twice" rule comes in. The first time I notice something or have an idea isn't the time to start shooting. But if I notice something and then notice it again later, it's probably time to pull the trigger.

The first time you think you have a brilliant thought, it may or may not be a good idea. The first time you see an issue may not be the time to address it. The second time you notice it, chances are much better that it's time to act. After the third and fourth time, you're just putting it off.

What sort of things am I talking about?

- Sharing a paradigm shift that will transform your work
- Embracing a new opportunity in ministry
- Volunteering for something that touches your heart
- Confronting an employee
- Inviting someone out on a date
- Requesting extra help from a faithful donor

In each of these scenarios, a misfire could be disastrous. Obviously, some situations call for immediate action. Other times require us to ask for God's strength to keep our mouths shut well beyond the second occurrence. This rule isn't foolproof, but it has certainly benefited me as I walk the line between self-control and my instinct to go. I've also learned to apply these three additional criteria, especially when I'm considering a confrontation:

- What is my motivation?
- Is it loving? (Note: loving isn't always the same as nice.)
- Is it beneficial?

So on Throwback Thursday, take time to reflect before acting on an idea or situation. If it's the second or third time you've thought it, filter it through these criteria. If it's still a green light, then do it!

2. Write down one thing you've learned in the past week.

Taking time to reflect on your day, discover lessons, and interact with God can be an incredibly beneficial spiritual discipline. But finding the time to do it can be difficult. So just write down one thing. That's doable. Don't make it complicated. Use a dedicated composition notebook, a file on your computer, or a notes app on your phone—whatever works best for you. Each week write down one valuable lesson you've learned and take a few minutes to review the ones from previous weeks.

The goal here isn't to simply create a list of greatest hits from each week; the purpose is to help you remember the great things you're learning so you can continue to apply and execute these lessons. Remember the story of Lucy from the beginning of the chapter? We don't want the memory of the things we're learning on our growth journey to get lost in the busyness of our lives. Anyone who's taken notes in a class or presentation or anyone who's forgotten an important meeting because it wasn't on the calendar knows that putting pen to paper significantly enhances our ability to recall information.

3. Reach out to someone you haven't talked to in the last ninety days.

Life gets hectic, people get busy, and important relationships get neglected. Neglect brings regret and regret brings guilt. Guilt then makes it even harder to reconnect. Throwback Thursday provides you with the motivation to sidestep the awkwardness and just reconnect. If you make fifty reconnections in the next year, you'll quickly be caught up on neglected relationships. Think how good that will feel! And then you can focus on staying connected.

This challenge is incredibly enriching to the soul, maybe because the impact is so long lasting. It's unbelievably satisfying to send an email to an old friend or colleague and get a response saying, "You have no idea how badly I needed that."

Take a moment and ask God to guide you down memory lane. Look through your contacts and pick someone who sticks out to you—maybe an old friend, family member, teacher, or someone else who meant a lot to you. Don't overthink it. Just choose a name that feels right. You always have next week to choose another name.

Now devote fifteen minutes to the person you selected. It could mean a call, an email, or even a letter. Just let them know what they mean to you, catch up, encourage them, or tell them you're praying for them. This is a small sacrifice of time, and it may pull you out of your comfort zone a little, but the payoff could be huge both for the person you reach out to and for you.

Moment of Grace

We can do nothing to earn grace. That's why it's a priceless gift. But we can choose to be gracious or ungracious recipients. Take another moment to reflect on God's goodness over the past week and respond with thanksgiving. Some weeks that will be easy. Other weeks, that may be hard. Notice what scripture says: "Give thanks to the LORD, for he is good; his love endures forever" (Psalm 118:1).

Being thankful is both an affirmation of God's current goodness and declaration of faith in his future love. The word for "love" here is *hesed*, which means "a covenantal or loyal love."[2] The best modern example of covenantal love is marriage. God's *hesed* reminds us that he committed to us forever, to love and cherish, to always protect and provide. Though even a healthy marriage can have its ups and downs, God's love is trustworthy, regardless of our current circumstances. Rest in his love this week, no matter how many challenges you complete.

Discussion Questions

1. Would you describe yourself as someone who struggles to speak up and offer feedback or someone who occasionally puts their foot in their mouth?

2. If you tend to hold back your feedback, what keeps you from speaking up?

3. If you tend to offer too much feedback or offer feedback too soon, what kind of filter do you need to help you make the most of your opportunities?

4. Are you more inclined to spend too much or too little time looking back? What are the advantages and disadvantages of each?

THROWBACK THURSDAY

When will you attempt your first Throwback Thursday?

_____

Track 1

- ☐ Apply the "think it twice" rule.

Track 2

- ☐ Apply the "think it twice" rule.
- ☐ Write down one thing you've learned in the past week.

Track 3

- ☐ Apply the "think it twice" rule.
- ☐ Write down one thing you've learned in the past week.
- ☐ Reach out to someone you haven't talked to in the last ninety days.

13

FINISH STRONG FRIDAY

A t the end of his life, the apostle Paul wrote:

> I have fought the good fight, I have finished the race, I have kept the faith. Now there is in store for me the crown of righteousness, which the Lord, the righteous Judge, will award to me on that day—and not only to me, but also to all who have longed for his appearing. (2 Timothy 4:7–8)

Contrast that to so many other biblical characters. David, Solomon, Samson, Gideon, and many more stumbled—sometimes spectacularly—before the finish line. It is much easier to start strong than to finish strong. Working with college students, I found that young people are especially great at starting things. I remember watching some of the players on my team excel at wooing a girl and starting a relationship in an extraordinary way, only to break up by text! Why? Because ending the relationship correctly was too hard. I loved my guys, so we had some hard conversations about having the courage to end things in a more honoring manner.

At the same time, finishing weak is hardly a young person's issue. Most of the biblical examples I just shared failed in their later years. As human beings, we're inherently better at starting than finishing. We start budgets, home improvement projects, diets, and Bible-reading programs (and leadership programs?) but struggle to stay on track. Starting only requires passion, while finishing requires grit and depth of character.

> *Starting only requires passion, while finishing*
> *requires grit and depth of character.*

If you are a high-capacity person, someone who was always at the head of the class, you may be especially prone to failed finishes. Talent and charisma can make it too easy to advance without forcing you to develop the stamina for going the distance. I don't say that to discourage you, but to exhort you. As you once devoted energy to getting ahead, now devote energy to finishing strong.

In studying high-impact ministry leaders, I saw they were consistently strong finishers. This is nonnegotiable. One way to develop the habit of finishing strong is by finishing each week strong. Think of the week as practice for your life. For many of us, Fridays are the least productive day of the week. However, I want you to build your endurance by sprinting across the finish line, just like I made my guys "run through the line" when we did our conditioning drills.

FINISH STRONG FRIDAY MINDSET
Friday Strong Friday is my day to sprint across the finish line. By pushing myself harder and completing more tasks, I will build my endurance and train myself to finish strong.

Coasting into the weekend may feel natural but will cost you the opportunity to continue building credibility and influence. Your team is watching you. Here are three ways you could finish every week strong.

1. Complete one task as though it were in front of a cheering crowd.

In this challenge, we're going to focus on finishing strong. But here I want to focus on the strong part. I like running races of all distances and have noticed that while a lot of spectators may gather at the starting line, they've thinned out by the midpoint. You see the runners adopt a comfortable pace, and some may drop out due to injuries or insufficient training. Then about a quarter mile from the finish line, the crowds start forming and the runners find just a little bit more to give. When they hear the cheering and see the photographers, they pick up their pace and cross the line in full stride.

In the Olympics, athletes devote a lifetime of effort for just one opportunity to compete. I want to encourage you to give an Olympian effort to one endeavor each week. Today, pick one thing—a class you teach, meeting you lead, mentoring conversation, sermon illustration, date with your spouse—and focus on investing your absolute best. Pretend you're about to cross the finish line in front of cheering spectators. If it's a date, make it better than your first date. If it's a sermon illustration, fine tune it as if it will be featured on *Preaching Today*. If it's a mentoring conversation, imagine it will impact the rest of their life, because it just might. If it's a meeting, treat it as if it will determine the future of your organization. If it's a class, act as if every parent and school board member were in the room.

I said to pretend you're doing it in front of a huge crowd, but it's not actually pretending. As the writer of Hebrews wrote:

Therefore, since we are surrounded by such a great cloud of witnesses, let us throw off everything that hinders and the sin that so easily entangles. And let us run with perseverance the race marked out for us, fixing our eyes on Jesus, the pioneer and perfecter of faith. (Hebrews 12:1–2)

We are running our race in front the angels, saints past and present, and our precious Savior. Run well, encouraged by Paul's words, "Always give yourselves fully to the work of the Lord, because you know that your labor in the Lord is not in vain" (1 Corinthians 15:58).

2. Finish as many things as possible.

On Monday, I said to devote your energy to three high-priority tasks and save the lower-priority tasks for the end of the week. Don't waste your creative energy, which is highest on Monday, on busywork. Keep punting it toward Friday when your creative energy may be running low. Well, it's Friday—time to tackle those lower-priority tasks.

Meredith is a compulsive list maker, and she loves to check the boxes. It is literally addictive. Completing a task—no matter how small—releases a hit of dopamine, making us want to do it again.[1] Pull out the list of lower-priority tasks, and challenge yourself to complete as many as possible. Start with quick ones to build momentum.

Even I'll admit this is where a to-do list can be useful. Fridays, for instance, are a great day for clearing out my inbox. If I can shut down my computer Friday afternoon with an empty inbox, I feel ready for the weekend. This one has had ripple effects in my organization. I've coached our whole team on this, so they know a Friday afternoon email to me will get a prompt response. Many organizations' emails go dead from two to five on Friday afternoons, but ours light up! We're excited to finish strong: get that contract done, call back that church, and finish sending out action steps. Don't coast into the weekend. Instead, find your second wind and burst across the finish line.

3. Give a specific affirmation to two people.

This is more than giving a compliment. Saying, "Nice work, Heather," is a compliment. An affirmation says, "Heather, you really served our client well today. The way you go the extra mile and exceed expectations is a great reflection on all of us. Thank you." What could have been a simple acknowledgment became an affirmation because you defined specifically what Heather did and why it was so valuable.

This challenge is similar to Monday's, but the difference is that this one focuses specifically on the people you lead or serve alongside. I've seen leaders who look down on affirmations, like a paycheck should be enough, and only needy people want affirmations. This lack of graciousness is a symptom of a withered soul and is at odds with the Bible. "Well done, good and faithful servant!" (Matthew 25:21) is held up as a noble affirmation that we should all seek. The apostle Paul, who wrote the most books of the New Testament, graciously acknowledged others at the end of almost every letter and even named Timothy and Silvanus as coauthors on several of his epistles. Genuine affirmations flow out of a leader's humility and generosity of soul. They are an amazing tool for leaders who want to build credibility and influence with those they serve.

> *Affirmations flow out of a leader's humility*
> *and generosity of soul.*

Not only do affirmations encourage those we lead; they also encourage the sort of behaviors we want to see from them. As parents, Ronda and I found that it was easy to focus on correcting wrong behaviors, but it was just as important to encourage what our kids did right.

One more thing—this is amazing—research shows that when a person receives an affirmation, it releases endorphins.[2] That's great. I'm glad to make my team happy. But scientists also discovered that giving an affirmation releases more endorphins than receiving one. Better to give than receive, indeed. What a great way to go into the weekend! Affirming two people and celebrating them in specific ways ends their week on a great note while also giving you a burst of energy.

Moment of Grace

Think back over your mistakes of the past week: the times you were selfish, didn't lead from a heart of love, and were filled with pride or doubt. Bring your failures and regrets to God. Clear your slate before going into the weekend, personally and with God and with those you get to serve.

> When you were dead in your sins and in the uncircumcision of your flesh, God made you alive with Christ. He forgave us all our sins, having canceled the charge of our legal indebtedness, which stood against us and condemned us; he has taken it away, nailing it to the cross. (Colossians 2:13–14)

With humility and gratitude, accept the grace that God pours out. His grace is more than enough to both erase your sin and heal the damage you may have done. Then ask yourself if you need to apologize to anyone. Leaders can set no greater example than to genuinely apologize for their own mistakes.

> *Leaders can set no greater example than to*
> *genuinely apologize for their own mistakes.*

Now take another moment to think about anyone who has wronged you. "Bear with each other and forgive one another if any of you has a grievance against someone. Forgive as the Lord forgave you" (Colossians 3:13). Even better than finishing your week with a completed to-do list is finishing it with "clean books"!

Discussion Questions

1. Looking back on your life, what is your approximate things-started to things-finished ratio? What factors usually lead to your quitting?

2. Have talent and charisma made starting easy for you? Whether you answered yes or no, how do you think that's affected your stamina?

3. Sometimes not finishing something demonstrates wisdom and prudence. How do you know when to push through and when to call it quits?

4. What are the low-value activities you put off throughout the week? If you began finishing strong and knocking out those to-dos, what value would that add to your life and to your ministry work?

5. What do people in your life say to you that makes you feel the most affirmed? What do they comment on? What phrases encourage you most?

6. Does giving affirmations to others come to you naturally, or is it something you have to work hard to do? How could giving two affirmations every week transform you and your team?

FINISH STRONG FRIDAY

When will you attempt your first Finish Strong Friday?

_____

Track 1

☐ Complete one task as though it were in front of a cheering crowd.

Track 2

☐ Complete one task as though it were in front of a cheering crowd.
☐ Finish as many things as possible.

Track 3

☐ Complete one task as though it were in front of a cheering crowd.
☐ Finish as many things as possible.
☐ Give a specific affirmation to two people.

CHAPTER

14

FILL YOUR TANK DAY

M y grandmother, Ellen Wells, lived across the street from my childhood home and played a crucial role in my life, especially after my father died. Every Saturday, she had her own ridiculous routine. First, she'd go to our local grocery store and fill her pantry. Then she'd go over to the gas station and fill her tank. It didn't matter if it was already seven-eighths full, she'd top it off. Finally, she'd go to Kay's, the local beauty shop.

Watching her go through her routine, I intuitively understood that the beauty shop filled her spirit the same way that she filled her pantry and car. She didn't just have her hair and nails done. Grandma Wells was a widow by that time, had also lost two of her children, and was alone most of the week. At the beauty shop she got with her girls and filled her friendship and fellowship tanks, swapping stories and catching up on the latest news. She left the beauty shop with a radiance that had nothing to do with her hair and nails.

Filling your own tank is one of your most important responsibilities as leaders. This is not NASCAR. You don't have a crew chief counting laps and making sure you've got tread on your tires and gas in your tank. You must be able to say, "It's time for me focus on myself." Does that sound selfish? I used to think so. Like many leaders, I led out of a deficit for far too long. I spent years making sure everyone else was taken care of while neglecting my health, my energy, and my family. The hard lesson I learned is that running on empty doesn't serve others well. Once I made a commitment to take a little time and direct it toward activities that fill my tank, I found that my ability to engage deeply, challenge appropriately, and serve passionately was greatly enhanced.

Think again of a NASCAR race. The entire time the car is in the pit stop, it seems to be falling behind. Car after car that it worked so hard to pass flies by. But what happens if the driver refuses to pull out? Either he's going to run out of gas or blow a tire, creating a very dangerous situation. Some people watch car races just to see such crashes. It's far less entertaining, however, when Christian leaders crash and burn, taking down others with them and deeply dishonoring the name of Jesus.

Moral failure is complex, and there is no one reason or cause, but neglecting to fill our own tank is a common factor. Why? Because we can only run on empty for so long. If we refuse to fill up in a healthy way, we're more likely to fill up in an unhealthy way. Even without a moral failure, many leaders who have run out of gas become victims of burnout. That may not be as dramatic or destructive, but it has cut short many a ministry and harmed the spouses and children of many leaders. Refusing to fill your tank is not sacrificial. It is selfish.

> *Refusing to fill your tank is not sacrificial. It is selfish.*

We've all seen or known leaders who ran out of gas or created a massive wreck on the track. It's vital to watch for the warning signs in yourself (or those around you). Here are some I've observed:

- You're becoming less patient. The fuse is shorter, and the explosion is bigger.
- Your enthusiasm is sagging.
- Your efficiency is declining. Things that used to take forty-five minutes now take a couple of hours.
- You find you're reacting to situations instead of being proactive.
- You're procrastinating and delegating tasks that you shouldn't.
- You're beginning to get caught up in low-value activities.
- You feel lethargic.
- Temptations are harder to resist.

The good news is that all of these are early warning signs. In some cases, you're just one restorative weekend away from being at 100 percent. The bad news is, the longer you ignore these symptoms, the longer they take to recover from.

Because the flow of the workweek can vary so much from situation to situation, I'm not going to delineate between Saturday and Sunday. I'll treat them as a group and allow you to determine how it works in your context. And if you are a pastor or on a church staff, Sunday may be a workday for you. Naming the days of the week is less about the actual day and more about establishing intentional rhythms. If Saturday or Sunday aren't your days of rest, simply apply these recommendations to the days that are.

Fill Your Tank Mindset

My time off is my time to refill my tank and restore my soul. By doing things that I enjoy and by intentionally resting, I increase both my dependency on God's grace and the resources I have to offer those I lead.

---

1. Enjoy a full, guilt-free day not working.

If you are already good at a work-life balance, calling this a challenge is almost laughable. But if your identity is rooted in what you do or if your calendar has filled to the point of overflowing, the idea of a day without checking your email, texting a coworker, or finishing up a project can be downright scary. A day without running errands or rushing between soccer games will seem impossible. Pay attention to what God teaches us about our day of rest through this story about manna:

> Each morning everyone gathered as much [manna] as they needed, and when the sun grew hot, it melted away. On the sixth day, they gathered twice as much—two omers for each person—and the leaders of the community came and reported this to Moses. He said to them, "This is what the LORD commanded: 'Tomorrow is to be a day of sabbath rest, a holy Sabbath to the LORD. So bake what you want to bake and boil what you want to boil. Save whatever is left and keep it until morning.'"
>
> So they saved it until morning, as Moses commanded, and it did not stink or get maggots in it. "Eat it today," Moses said, "because today is a sabbath to the LORD. You will not find any of it on the ground today. Six days you are to gather it, but on the seventh day, the Sabbath, there will not be any."
>
> Nevertheless, some of the people went out on the seventh day to gather it, but they found none. Then the LORD said to Moses, "How long

will you refuse to keep my commands and my instructions? Bear in mind that the LORD has given you the Sabbath; that is why on the sixth day he gives you bread for two days. Everyone is to stay where they are on the seventh day; no one is to go out." So the people rested on the seventh day. (Exodus 16:21–30)

It's easy to joke about being a workaholic, but God didn't see the Israelites' attempts at Sabbath manna gathering as amusing or even as good stewardship. He called it disobedience.

You've probably heard, or given, many sermons saying tithing reminds us that all our money belongs to God. In the same way, the Sabbath rest is our reminder that all our time, all our energy, and all our work belong to him. Taking a day of rest embraces God's grace, trusting that he will provide us with more fruitfulness in six days than we could naturally achieve in seven.

It's up to you to decide what your Sabbath rest looks like but allow it to be a time to enjoy resting without guilt. This may feel radical or uncomfortable. It's certainly countercultural. But God established a rhythm of work and rest at creation. Embracing one without the other robs us of his intentional design.

Some people find it useful to follow the Old Testament's system of sundown to sundown. For instance, even if you work a regular Monday through Friday workweek, you may find Saturday taken up by various home projects and other responsibilities. Begin your Sabbath rest on Saturday night and continue it through the following evening. Then, Sunday night, go through any emails that accumulated and plan out your Move the Needle Monday. For some of you, a full day to rest is not possible, so you may need to consider something like a weekly technology fast where you turn off your devices for a portion of the weekend. Even a few hours of rest every single week could be the Sabbath rest you need.

2. Discover and prioritize things that fill your tank.

Grandma Wells went to the beauty shop to fill up her tank. But if I had to sit in a chair and let somebody fiddle with my hair for ninety minutes, my patience would disappear, and my tank would have many holes in it. What's refreshing will be different for everyone, and that's more than okay. If you're an extrovert, hanging out with friends will fill you up. If you're an introvert, that will siphon off the little you had in your tank.

You probably already have a sense of your tank fillers but give yourself the freedom to experiment. If you try something and think, *Why don't I do this more often?* then you've probably found a new tank filler. It could be dinner with a specific set of friends, lunch with a fun coworker, or a night out of town with your spouse. It could be virtually anything. Exercise, volunteering, reading, and so on. Once you've discovered your tank fillers, intentionally engage in them as a discipline of joy. Deliberately plan for them, even if it means adjusting or eliminating other activities.

3. Invest in a tank-filling friendship.

Throughout this book I have been consistently clear that leadership is defined by our service to others. We labor and strive to instruct, inspire, and influence people. Our goal is the success of others. Friendship is defined by a mutual service, as scripture tells us: "Therefore encourage one another and build each other up, just as in fact you are doing" (1 Thessalonians 5:11). Every high-impact leader I know has deep friendships that result in mutual encouragement, tender transparency, and joy-filled fellowship.

Tank-filling relationships include three characteristics:

- Mutual encouragement: Does this friend encourage and build you up as much as you build them up?
- Acceptance: Are you free to be yourself with this friend? Can you truly pour out your heart to them? Can you and your spouse get into a disagreement in their presence?
- Enjoyment: Do you honestly enjoy your time with this friend?

I know that relationships like this are few and far between, but you need a place where you can be fully human. Cultivating these relationships well will involve intentionality. After all, these are the people who bring great value to our lives, so we need to be sure that we are connecting with them—and bringing value to them—often. These relationships will also require investment. In relationships where we will make emotional withdrawals, we must be mindful to pour back into them by sharing our deepest appreciation and affirmation for these precious relationships.

Moment of Grace

I said that filling our tanks is a discipline of joy, and I'm borrowing that concept from Josh Kelley, author of *Radically Normal: You Don't Have to Live Crazy to Follow Jesus.* Josh wrote:

> Joy is one of the central themes of the Bible. When I was doing research for this book, I did an extensive study on the word *joy* and its synonyms, including *happiness, pleasure,* and *delight.* I trimmed the list down to the 730 most applicable verses containing those words. That's a lot of verses— more than the number of verses that contain words like *peace, grace,* or even *love.*[1]

He goes on to say that roughly one-third of these joys comes from earthly things, like a good meal or delighting in creation. Josh's point is the Bible invites us to enjoy all God's many good gifts. Embrace God's gift of rest and be refreshed by his grace, just like Jesus invites us to do:

> Come to me, all you who are weary and burdened, and I will give you rest. Take my yoke upon you and learn from me, for I am gentle and humble in heart, and you will find rest for your souls. For my yoke is easy and my burden is light. (Matthew 11:28–30)

Discussion Questions

1. On a scale from one to ten—with one being "I never really get or take a day off and can't imagine how I could," and ten being "I maximize my time off by doing only the things that really fill my tank"—where are you when it comes to enjoying your time off?

2. When you take time off from ministry work, do you feel free, guilt, or a mix of both? Why do you think those are the feelings you experience during your time off?

3. List at least three life-giving, soul-nurturing activities that bring you joy.

4. How can tank-filling days positively impact you, those you love, and your ministry?

FILL YOUR TANK DAY

When will you attempt your first Fill Your Tank Day?

Track 1

☐ Enjoy a full, guilt-free day not working.

Track 2

☐ Enjoy a full, guilt-free day not working.
☐ Discover and prioritize things that fill your tank.

Track 3

☐ Enjoy a full, guilt-free day not working.
☐ Discover and prioritize things that fill your tank.
☐ Invest in a tank-filling friendship.

CHAPTER

15

COMPOUNDING
LEADERSHIP

During my first year as athletic director at Palm Beach Atlantic University, we had a few student athletes get into some minor trouble on campus and in the community. This is not atypical of a collegiate athletic program, but one troubling issue for me was that many of the players who were involved in these issues were team captains. At a staff meeting near the end of that first year, I asked the head coaches in our department how they selected their team captains. Their answer surprised me.

"We look for the best player. Or a senior," they said.

The lightbulb immediately clicked on in my head. Neither age nor athletic ability magically gives a player leadership skills. We were asking these kids to lead and giving them authority but not equipping them. That's like sending a soldier into battle with a butter knife. I began holding a weekly meeting, the "Captains' Club," to teach them foundational leadership principles. The effect was almost immediate. We saw team captains growing in their awareness of their influence, taking more responsibility for their behavior, and becoming more intentional about the team culture and chemistry. We added a monthly "blue and white night" (our school colors) to teach leadership lessons to all our student athletes. I quickly found myself underresourced and suddenly became a very serious, and motivated, student of leadership. I spent hours reading John Maxwell, Stephen Covey, and Flip Flippen. I studied scripture to find biblical leadership principles. I listened to countless cassettes (yes, cassettes!) on leadership.

As our student athletes became more competent in their leadership, we partnered with other organizations on campus— student life, student government, residential life, student missions, and other groups. This resulted in a robust annual student leadership retreat, and to this day, PBAU continues to make leadership a major emphasis.

Initially, I faced resistance from some of my captains. Their attitude was, *I don't want to lead. I don't want to attend a frivolous meeting. I don't want to be responsible for my teammates. I'm just here to play. Let me show up and play ball.* But I made it clear that, as Christians, that wasn't an option. We taught them that their goal was the success of others. They might be seniors on their way out, but behind them were freshman, sophomores, and juniors who needed guidance. It was their job to raise up the next generation of leaders. That's what great organizations, and great leaders, do: they generously duplicate themselves.

> *Great leaders generously duplicate themselves.*

When I travel and invest into leaders, my wife will often ask me about the number of people that I spoke to. That's a layered question, because the number of people in attendance and the number of people influenced can be greatly different. If the number of people in attendance apply the leadership principles that I taught, if they become true leaders and duplicate themselves, then the number of people influenced could be three, five, or even ten times greater than the number of people in attendance.

In chapter 6, I talked about the power of compounding habits. Now I want to shift to the power of compounding leadership. Compounding leadership is the effect of seeing your growth and investment in others travel beyond your immediate sphere of influence. It's the ripple effect of strong, healthy leadership and not all that different from the mission Jesus gave the disciples before he returned to heaven: "You will be my witnesses in Jerusalem, and in all Judea and Samaria, and *to the ends of the earth*" (Acts 1:8, emphasis added).

Compounding leadership is exciting and rewarding to witness, and I believe it is our calling. But it can also come at a cost. Many times, I've had the privilege of working with dynamic, talented women and men who led with high credibility and strong influence. Our organization had invested generously in them, and it had paid off, exponentially. We wanted them to stay a part of our team for a very long time. But at some point, they were offered an opportunity elsewhere and felt led to embrace it. Accepting the resignations of incredible leaders always creates a rare combination of sorrow and joy. We are sad to lose them, but at the same time couldn't be happier for them. We know the new opportunities will allow them to stretch their skill sets in new ways and influence others in new areas. And while they will be greatly missed, we cheer them on as they begin working their way "to the ends of the earth."

An example of compounding leadership can be seen in the sports world. One characteristic of all great athletic coaches is that they develop "coaching trees." They have a legacy of developing other leaders who go on to lead other organizations well. Coach Mike Krzyzewski, the winningest college basketball coach of all time, had twelve former assistants who have become head coaches. Nick Saban, the most successful college football coach of his generation, has developed multiple head coaches in both the college and professional ranks. Not only have Krzyzewski's and Saban's compounding leadership resulted in multiple new coaches, but it's spread their influence across multiple teams that will then influence dozens or even hundreds more players over the years.

Though it can be hard to lose good leaders, I want to practice compounding leadership. Rather than holding tight to everyone with potential and importance to me personally, I want to generously train up great leaders and happily send them out to train more leaders themselves. Rather than putting my trust in people and fearing they can never be replaced, I want to operate out of an abundance mentality and trust God to provide someone to step into their role. I want to do more than increase my leadership; I want to compound it.

My dear friend Marlene Ostrom and her late husband were missionaries in the Philippines, where they established a thriving church. When a family tragedy forced them to come home and take over her family's business, God gave them the opportunity to use that business to fund the training of Filipino pastors and the building of new churches. They could have lamented the loss of their mission and assumed their influence had come to an end, but they chose to trust God and hold their resources and their expectations loosely. Instead of planting just one church themselves, they were able to fund more than a thousand churches and watch their influence reach more than they ever could have alone.

I want compounding leadership like that! That's why I do what I do and why I wrote this book. I want to influence—and leadership is simply influencing—thousands of leaders who go on to influence millions. My heart is to influence you so that you will become the compounding leaders who influence your campus, your church, your city, and our world in a way that honors God and transforms others.

———

My hope is *The Five-Day Leader* will help you develop habits that not only build your credibility and influence but are compounded through everyone you lead. Every time you choose to practice Move the Needle Monday, Tough Tuesday, WOW Wednesday, Throwback Thursday, and Finish Strong Friday, you will grow in new ways and the people you lead will be directly influenced by your intentionality.

My prayer is that we would be used by God in ways that are radical and disproportionate to who we are. It is in God's grace and power that we serve. May we do it all for his purposes and to his pleasure.

EPILOGUE

In God's unique design, he created us to be relational and influential in the lives of others. We see throughout scripture times where the potential for influence was stewarded well and times that it wasn't. My prayer is that you and your teams would use the 5-Day Leader process so we can all steward our influence well.

You have been called by God into a global movement of men and women who are committed to impacting the world by advancing the gospel and sharing the love and lessons of Jesus Christ. We don't have time to waste. Now is the time to start implementing the tools offered in *The Five-Day Leader* because they have the potential to bless and benefit everyone around you.

One of the pictures on my prayer board is of a launching pad at the Kennedy Space Center. It's a metaphor for leadership that challenges me every day. Let me explain.

The space program started in October 1958. The first initiative was Mercury (six missions), followed by Gemini (nineteen missions), and then Apollo (eleven missions). All these programs had spacecraft that were for single use. The rockets were built for a single mission and retired following that mission. In the 1980s NASA shifted to the Space Shuttle program. Six spacecraft were built with the intention of being multiuse, with each shuttle going into space multiple times. In total the program completed 135 shuttle missions, with the space shuttle *Discovery* being the most prolific by flying a total of thirty-nine missions.

The fascinating thing to me is that all these space missions, every single one, originated on just a few launching pads at the Kennedy Space Center in Florida.

As I dream about the leadership influence I want you to have, consider the fact that some leaders are like the rockets in the Mercury, Gemini, and Apollo missions—they have a single season of significant influence. Apollo missions landed men on the moon, but their influence was reserved for a single season, with a relatively narrow impact. Other leaders are like a space shuttle—they are influential multiple times, in various seasons, but ultimately their impact is still a bit minimized.

I want to challenge you and your teams to be like a launchpad. Launchpads were the origin of every single mission launched at the Kennedy Space Center. In fact, the launchpads that were in use for the moon missions in the 1960s are now launching SpaceX rockets today.

A launchpad leader has influence in every season of their life, with multiple areas of impact, and they exist to equip and encourage other leaders toward their calling, passion, and mission. Simply put, launchpad leaders launch others.

My prayer every day for myself, my team, and for you reading this book is that we will become launchpad leaders, using the skills and strategies that are in these pages to influence others on a trajectory that will take them further and faster than they ever dreamed they could go.

I invite you to join the 5-Day Leader movement around the world so you can grow your leadership skills, influence others, and impact the world for Christ. It's been my honor to influence you, and now it's your time to launch. The countdown has begun.

5 ... 4 ... 3 ... 2 ... 1

The Five-Day Leader Process

	Track 1	Track 2	Track 3
Move the Needle Monday	❑ Engage one Truth Teller and ask for their feedback.	❑ Engage one Truth Teller and ask for their feedback. ❑ Define your three highest-value activities for the week and write them down in order of priority.	❑ Engage one Truth Teller and ask for their feedback. ❑ Define your three highest-value activities for the week and write them down in order of priority. ❑ Celebrate two people in your life, or in the life of someone you care about.
Tough Tuesday	❑ Add one hour to your day and devote it to your growth.	❑ Add one hour to your day and devote it to your growth. ❑ The Plus-One Challenge: push yourself to "add one" to whatever you do today.	❑ Add one hour to your day and devote it to your growth. ❑ The Plus-One Challenge: push yourself to "add one" to whatever you do today. ❑ Say "no" or "not yet" to at least one task, request, opportunity, or invitation, and invest the time saved into the relationships that matter most.

WOW Wednesday	❑ Find one way to make the people you serve say, "Wow!"	❑ Find one way to make the people you serve say, "Wow!" ❑ Try something new that takes you way out of your comfort zone.	❑ Find one way to make the people you serve say, "Wow!" ❑ Try something new that takes you way out of your comfort zone. ❑ Give a gift to build a relationship.
Throwback Thursday	❑ Apply the "think it twice" rule.	❑ Apply the "think it twice" rule. ❑ Write down one thing you've learned in the past week.	❑ Apply the "think it twice" rule. ❑ Write down one thing you've learned in the past week. ❑ Reach out to someone you haven't talked to in the last ninety days.
Finish Strong Friday	❑ Complete one task as though it were in front of a cheering crowd.	❑ Complete one task as though it were in front of a cheering crowd. ❑ Finish as many things as possible.	❑ Complete one task as though it were in front of a cheering crowd. ❑ Finish as many things as possible. ❑ Give a specific affirmation to two people.

ACKNOWLEDGMENTS

I encourage leaders to have both a purpose statement and a process statement. My process statement is to "do hard things with people I really care about and have fun doing it." This project was certainly a great example of living my process statement. Getting a book published is a hard thing! The people who came alongside to encourage and support this process are people I deeply care about, and I had a great time throughout this process.

Ronda, Michael, and Jordie, I know that every time I say yes to something there is a sacrifice from our family, yet each of you showed your own strength, persistence, and commitment to growth with each opportunity. No man has lived his life surrounded by as much love, loyalty, and laughter as I have. I love each of you unconditionally, cherish you deeply, and wouldn't trade you for anything in the world. Your inspiration and influence are the reasons this book exists.

When scripture says that "it is not good for the man to be alone," I am living proof. When I introduce people to my wife, Ronda, I tell them that she's everything that I am not. I am not a lot of things, but God has gifted me with a partner who has willingly jumped into every adventure with all her heart, all her strength, and with all her support. Thank you, Ronda. There has never been a better counselor or a bigger cheerleader than you.

Our prayer for our children was that God would raise up

children with passion, as well as the character and work ethic to support it. The most important leadership platform a leader has is in their home. Thank you, Michael and Jordie, for becoming leaders who are both an example and an inspiration to me.

Meredith King has been my teacher, my Truth Teller, and my trustee from the very beginning of this process. Her enthusiasm and belief in this project often exceeded my own. Her commitment to this dream of mine is one of the most humbling acts of friendship that I have ever experienced.

Kat Armstrong has come alongside as a coach and coordinator of this project. I have been around great coaches all my life, but few have had the wisdom, experience, energy, and heart that Kat has demonstrated in this process. I am so amazed by her humility and heart to serve so selflessly in so many ways.

Flip and Susan Flippen have been my friends, my mentors, and two of the greatest supporters of this work and our family. These two incredible people have set a standard of excellence, generosity, and love that has challenged me and inspired me from the first time I met them. My appreciation for their contributions to my life is only exceeded by my admiration for them.

General Van, you provided equal parts wisdom and encouragement as this book was developing. You are the consummate example of credibility and influence.

Josh Kelley was my patient partner in this entire process. I believe that the greatest teacher we can have is the experience of another. Josh's experience in this business, his excellence as a writer, and wisdom as an editor have been invaluable. Josh helped to bring the book I had in me onto the written page.

Mary Carver and Patty Crowley Brown strengthened this project with their amazing editing skills. Thank you both for all your hard work.

Heather Seibel is one those unique people who lives to see others succeed. From her time at ESPN as an executive producer to her roles at Integrus, she simply makes every person and every process she engages with better. Her role in moving this project from dream to done is another example of her ability to make hard things easy.

Marta Hedde was my high school journalism teacher. She taught me to love the written word and showed how a true leader builds influence and credibility with a team. It has always been my dream to honor her impact on my life by writing a book.

The time I had with both my mother and father was way too short, but their love and lessons are with me each day. Mom and Dad, I love you, I miss you, and much of the common sense found on these pages came from you.

Finally, *all* my teammates at Integrus have contributed to this work in many ways. The lessons I have learned from you and the lives you lead have influenced every word of this book. Thank you all so very much.

NOTES

Chapter 1: Overwhelmed and Underresourced

1. Julie Maxwell, "Why Pastors Leave the Ministry," *Shepherds Watchmen*, August 11, 2019, https://shepherdswatchmen.com/browse-all-posts/why-pastors-leave-the-ministry/.
2. Bo Lane, "Why Do So Many Pastors Leave the Ministry? The Facts Will Shock You," *ExPastors*, January 27, 2014, http://www.expastors.com/why-do-so-many-pastors-leave-the-ministry-the-facts-will-shock-you/.
3. Chris Strub, "45% of Nonprofit Employees to Seek New Jobs by 2025: Report." *Forbes*, February 10, 2020, https://www.forbes.com/sites/chrisstrub/2020/02/10/nonprofithr/.
4. Brett Zeck, "You Will Touch 80,000 Lives," *Desiring God*, January 4, 2017, https://www.desiringgod.org/articles/you-will-touch-80000-lives.

Chapter 2: Five Crippling Myths

1. Peter Weir, director, *Dead Poets Society*, Touchstone Pictures, 1989. 2 hr., 8 min., https://www.imdb.com/title/tt0097165/.

Chapter 3: Five-Minute Definition

1. Tony Scott, director, *Top Gun*, Paramount Pictures, 1986, 1 hr., 50 min., https://www.imdb.com/title/tt0092099/.

Chapter 4: People Need Leaders

1. Marcus Buckingham, *The One Thing You Need to Know About Managing, Great Leading, and Sustained Individual Success* (New York: Free Press, 2005).
2. Ibid.
3. C. S. Lewis, *That Hideous Strength* (London: The Bodley Head, 1945).

Chapter 5: Relentless Growth

1. *Merriam-Webster*, s.v. "confrontation (*n.*)," accessed April 2, 2022, https://www.merriam-webster.com/dictionary/confrontation.

Chapter 7: Resilient Relationships

1. Jim Collins, *Good to Great: Why Some Companies Make the Leap and Others Don't* (New York: Harper Business, 2001).

Chapter 9: Move the Needle Monday

1. Chad Brooks, "The Most Productive Day of the Workweek Is …," *Business News Daily*, December 8, 2021, https://www.businessnewsdaily.com/5637-the-most-productive-day-of-the-workweek-may-surprise-you.html.
2. James Clear, *Atomic Habits: An Easy & Proven Way to Build Good Habits & Break Bad Ones* (New York: Avery, 2018).

Chapter 10: Tough Tuesday

1. https://www.n2growth.com/the-learning-ceo/

Chapter 11: WOW Wednesday

1. Tom Connellan, *Inside the Magic Kingdom: Seven Keys to Disney's Success* (Colorado Springs: Peak Performance, 1997).
2. Marianne Williamson, *A Return to Love: Reflections on the Principles of "A Course in Miracles"* (New York: Harper One, 2009), 191.

Chapter 12: Throwback Thursday

1. Peter Segal, director, *50 First Dates,* Happy Madison Productions, 2004, 1 hr., 39 min., https://www.imdb.com/title/tt0343660/.
2. *Blue Letter Bible*, s.v. "hesed" (*n*.), accessed April 2, 2022, https://www.blueletterbible.org/lexicon/h2617/niv/wlc/0-1/.

Chapter 13: Finish Strong Friday

1. Ralph Ryback, M.D., "The Science of Accomplishing Your Goals," Psychology Today, October 3, 2016, https://www.psychologytoday.com/us/blog/the-truisms-wellness/201610/the-science-accomplishing-your-goals.
2. Debbie Hampton, "The Neuroscience of How Affirmations Help Your Mental Health," The Best Brain Possible, November 22, 2019, https://thebestbrainpossible.com/affirmations-brain-depression-anxiety/.

Chapter 14: Fill Your Tank Day

1. Josh Kelley, *Radically Normal: You Don't Have to Live Crazy to Follow Jesus* (Eugene: Harvest House, 2014), 82.

Epilogue

1. www.nasa.gov
2. www.space.com

ABOUT THE AUTHOR

Lyle Wells is on a mission to ignite disciple makers as a trusted advisor, chief encourager, and leadership coach. His passion is to help develop healthy ministry leaders who accelerate their kingdom impact. Lyle's kids, his wife, and the thousands of high-caliber leaders he's invested in will tell you the same thing: you want Lyle in your corner. As a leading voice for high-impact kingdom builders, he is captivating a hundred audiences around the world every year. He spent decades transforming athletic programs and serving as a leader in higher education. Lyle's ministry experience includes serving as a senior pastor, church planter, and an executive senior pastor at one of the largest churches in the nation. Lyle is the president of Integrus Leadership, a published author, and an in-demand speaker and preacher. A devoted husband and present father, Lyle has been married to Ronda for thirty-two years, and together they love creating spontaneous family fun with their two grown children, Michael and Jordie.

@leadwithlyle
@integrusleadership
www.integrus.org

What kind of Leader are you?

Every leader has strengths and constraints. We're passionate about helping you identify them so that you can level up. Take our **12 Question Leadership Assessment** to discover where you are in your journey of leadership and what you can do to **find breakthrough**.

Take the Assessment:
Integrus.org/assessment

integrus
leadership

Catalyzing Ministry Leaders for Greater Kingdom Impact

Now more than ever, our world needs **healthy and effective ministry leaders**—that's how to advance the Kingdom. Get equipped to lead with confidence so you can **accelerate** your impact, **grow** your ministry and **transform** your community.

 ALIGNMENT 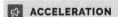 ACCELERATION 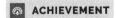 ACHIEVEMENT

 AWARENESS 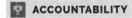 ACCOUNTABILITY

Scale Your Influence

 integrus.org
@integrusleadership

Printed in the United States
by Baker & Taylor Publisher Services